CARYL CH

Serious Money

with commentary and notes by
BILL NAISMITH

METHUEN DRAMA

Methuen Drama Student Edition

10 9 8 7 6 5 4 3 2 1

This edition first published in the United Kingdom in 2002 by
Methuen Publishing Ltd

Reissued with additional material and a new cover design in 2006

Methuen Drama
A & C Black Publishers Ltd
38 Soho Square, London W1D 3HB

Serious Money first published in 1987 by Methuen London in association
with the Royal Court Theatre. Revised and reissued in 1990

A CIP catalogue record for this book is available from the British Library

ISBN 0–413–77120–2
978–0–413–77120–9

Typeset by Deltatype Ltd, Birkenhead, Merseyside
Printed and bound in Great Britain by Bookmarque Ltd, Croydon

Contents

I should like to acknowledge the help and advice of the following friends in the preparation of this edition: Anthony Cunningham, Steven Dykes, Geoffrey James, Nesta Jones, Michael O'Grady, Brian Singleton, Alan Smith, and Peter Temple.

Bill Naismith

Caryl Churchill

1938 Born in London, 3 September.
1948–55 Lived in Montreal, Canada.
1957–60 Read English Language and Literature at Lady Margaret Hall, Oxford. Obtained B.A. in English.
1958 Student production at Oxford of *Downstairs* (one-act play), which went to the *Sunday Times*/National Union of Students Drama Festival in 1959.
1960 Student production of *Having a Wonderful Time* at The Questors Theatre, Ealing.
1961 Married David Harter, 20 May. Student production of *Easy Death* at the Oxford Playhouse. Student sound production of *You've No Need to be Frightened*.
1962 *The Ants* broadcast on the BBC Third Programme, 27 November, directed by Michael Bakewell.
1963 Son, Joe Harter, born on 26 April.
1964 Son, Paul Harter, born on 5 December.
1967 *Lovesick* broadcast on the BBC Third Programme, 2 May, directed by John Tydeman.
1968 *Identical Twins* broadcast on the BBC Third Programme, 21 November, directed by John Tydeman.
1969 Son, Rick Harter, born on 30 September.
1971 *Abortive* broadcast on the BBC Third Programme, 4 February, directed by John Tydeman. *Not . . . not . . . not . . . not . . . not enough oxygen* broadcast on the BBC Third Programme, 31 March, directed by John Tydeman.
1972 *Schreber's Nervous Illness* broadcast on the BBC Third Programme, 25 July, directed by John Tydeman. Lunchtime stage production, King's Head Theatre, London, 5 December 1972. *The Judge's Wife* televised on BBC TV, 2 October, directed by James Fermin. *Henry's Past* broadcast on the BBC Third Programme, 5 December, directed by John Tydeman. First production of *Owners*, Royal Court Theatre Upstairs, London, 6 December, directed by Nicholas Wright.

1973 *Perfect Happiness* broadcast on the BBC Third Programme, 30 September, directed by John Tydeman. Lunchtime stage production, Soho Poly, London, 10 March 1975, directed by Susanna Capon.

1974 –75 Resident dramatist at the Royal Court Theatre, London.

1974 *Turkish Delight*, televised on BBC TV, 22 April, directed by Herbert Wise.

1975 First production of *Objections to Sex and Violence*, Royal Court Theatre, 2 January, directed by John Tydeman. Sunday night Theatre Upstairs production of *Moving Clocks Go Slow*, 15 June, directed by John Ashford.

1976 *Light Shining in Buckinghamshire* with Joint Stock Theatre Group, directed by Max Stafford-Clark. Opened at the Traverse Theatre, Edinburgh, 7 September, and at the Royal Court Theatre Upstairs, 21 September. *Vinegar Tom* with Monstrous Regiment, directed by Pam Brighton. Opened at the Humberside Theatre, Hull, 12 October, and at the ICA, London, 6 December.

1977 First production of *Traps*, Royal Court Theatre Upstairs, 27 January, directed by John Ashford.

1978 Contributed with Michelene Wandor and Bryony Lavery to Monstrous Regiment's cabaret, *Floorshow*, which opened at the Theatre Royal, Stratford East, 18 January. *The After Dinner Joke* televised on BBC TV, 14 February, directed by Colin Bucksey. *The Legion Hall Bombing* televised on BBC TV, 22 August, directed by Roland Joffe. (At their request, Caryl Churchill's and Roland Joffe's names were removed from the credits.)

1979 *Cloud Nine* with Joint Stock Theatre Group, directed by Max Stafford-Clark. Opened at Dartington College of Arts, Devon, 14 February, and at the Royal Court Theatre, 29 March. Revival: Royal Court, September 1980, directed by Max Stafford-Clark and Les Waters. American production: Theatre de Lys, New York, 18 May 1981, directed by Tommy Tune.

1980 First production of *Three More Sleepless Nights*, Soho Poly, London, (lunchtime) 9 June, directed by Les Waters. Transferred to the Theatre Upstairs, August 1980.

1982 *Crimes* televised on BBC TV, 13 April, directed by Stuart Burge. First production of *Top Girls*, Royal Court Theatre,

28 August, directed by Max Stafford-Clark. Transferred to Joseph Papp's Public Theatre, New York, December 1982. Returned to the Royal Court, February 1983.

1983 *Fen* with Joint Stock Theatre Group, directed by Les Waters. Opened at the University of Essex Theatre, Colchester, 20 January, and at the Almeida Theatre, London, 16 February. Transferred to Joseph Papp's Public Theatre, New York, in May, and to the Royal Court Theatre, London, in July.

1984 First production of *Softcops*, Barbican Pit, London, 2 January, directed by Howard Davies. Contributed with Geraldine Pilgrim, Pete Brooks and John Ashford to *Midday Sun*, which opened at the ICA, London, 8 May.

1986 *A Mouthful of Birds* with Joint Stock Theatre Group, written by Caryl Churchill and David Lan, choreographed by Ian Spink, directed by Ian Spink and Les Waters. Opened at Birmingham Repertory Theatre, 2 September, and at the Royal Court Theatre, 25 November.

1987 First production of *Serious Money*, Royal Court Theatre, 21 March, directed by Max Stafford-Clark. Transferred to Wyndham's Theatre, London, July 1987, and to Joseph Papp's Public Theatre, New York, November 1987.

1988 Contributed to *Fugue, Dance on 4*, choreographed and directed by Ian Spink, televised on Channel 4, 26 June.

1989 First production of *Ice Cream*, Royal Court Theatre, 6 April, directed by Max Stafford-Clark.
Rehearsed reading of *Hot Fudge*, Royal Court Theatre, 11 May.

1990 First production of *Mad Forest*, Central School of Speech and Drama, London, 25 June, directed by Mark Wing-Davey.
Transferred to the National Theatre of Romania in Bucharest for two weeks before opening at the Royal Court, London in October.

1991 First production of *Lives of the Great Poisoners*, written for Second Stride Dance Company, choreographed and directed by Ian Spink, performed at the Riverside Studios in March.

1994 First production of *The Skriker*, Cottesloe, Royal National Theatre, 27 January, directed by Les Waters.
First production of *Thyestes* (translation of Seneca),

Manchester and Royal Court Theatre Upstairs, 7 June, directed by James Macdonald.

1997 First production of *Hotel*, with music by Orlando Gough and choreographed by Ian Spink, Second Stride, The Place, London, 17 April.

First production of *This is a Chair*, Royal Court Theatre, 25 June, directed by Stephen Daldry.

1997 &99 *Blue Heart* (*Heart's Desire* and *Blue Kettle*), produced by Out of Joint, directed by Max Stafford-Clark, Edinburgh Festival, Royal Court Theatre, London, New York and international tour.

2000 –1 *Far Away*, Royal Court Theatre Upstairs and Albery Theatre, London, 24 November, directed by Stephen Daldry.

2002 *A Number*, Royal Court Theatre, directed by Stephen Daldry (wins the *Evening Standard* Award for Best New Play).

2004 *A Number*, with New York Theatre Workshop, directed by James Macdonald.

Commentary

Background

Reactions to Thatcherism

Serious Money is widely regarded as a key play of the 1980s, an era inescapably linked with *Thatcherism*. In its depiction of rampant consumerism and heartless greed Churchill's play was extremely successful in London where it obviously struck a chord in 1986, not perhaps the best of times.

Mrs Thatcher was the first woman to lead the Conservative Party and the first woman to become Prime Minister of the United Kingdom (in 1979). She was re-elected in 1983 and 1987 and resigned in 1990. However, her sex was incidental to the political economy that guided her policies and profoundly affected the country and its people. The 1980s have been well documented and widely commented on, not least in the drama of the time which portrays a period of unprecedented greed, self-promoting individualism and a general assault on culture. Before reflecting on how artists and observers reacted to the period it is probably wise to revise and consider what Thatcher and her government did and why.

Margaret Thatcher came to power at a time of recession, following a wave of highly unpopular strikes by public service workers throughout Britain. She, and her favoured advisers, chose the economics of monetarism to combat this and restore national growth. The theory had been espoused in the USA by Professor Milton Friedman, who argued that 'Inflation is always and everywhere a monetary phenomenon' (*Dollars and Deficits*, Prentice-Hall, 1968). Monetarist policy requires the curbing of the money supply and the raising of interest rates in order to reduce inflation. By making borrowing more expensive through higher interest rates, total demand for goods and services will be eased and price rises will slow down. Perhaps for the first time since World War Two, full employment ceased to be a British Government priority. In fact unemployment was an essential factor in the plan to curb wage rises and costs, and thereby make British industry more competitive (unemployment was a little over two million in 1980; by December 1981 it had reached a record three million). Government spending was to be curtailed (£500 million was cut in 1983 – £140 million from the Health Service) and public corporations were to be 'rationalised' – i.e. streamlined, and, where possible, privatised (British Airways, British Telecom, the coal, gas, electricity, iron and steel industries, etc.).

These policies had the effect of decimating manufacturing industry. The consequences were clearly evident in an ever widening divide between an impoverished North of Britain and a prosperous South.

It became a tenet of Conservative policy that people should look less to the government for help and more to individual enterprise and initiative. For this reason, Margaret Thatcher applauded the new enterprise culture of the City. Of the young dealers whom Churchill exposes so damningly in *Serious Money*, Thatcher was to say:

> The City's growing confidence and drive owes a good deal to young people. Its vast new dealing rooms are run by the young: people who have made it not because of who they know or what school tie they wear, but on sheer merit, and that is the kind of society I want to see. (London, 1986)

The social consequences of these economic policies, as they affected ordinary people, were given vivid articulation by dramatists in the eighties. *Serious Money* is entirely a response to Thatcherism, each Act ending with a resounding and wholly ironic chorus in her praise. Churchill's own *Top Girls* (1982) and David Hare's *The Secret Rapture* (1988) show the all-pervading influence of Thatcherism throughout the decade. Both plays have two sisters at their centre, one of whom argues for the 'new Conservatism' while the other represents different values. In Hare's play Marion is a Conservative junior minister. Her sister Isobel lacks all competitive edge. Their stepmother Katherine, newly widowed, is becoming a liability.

> MARION. It's just the time. You must feel it. It's out there. It's the only thing I regret about belonging to the Government. Unfortunately I've got to help drive the gravy train. I'd rather be clambering on the back and joining in the fun.
> ISOBEL. What fun?
> MARION. Making money.

KATHERINE. Darling, everybody is.
MARION. Please wake up.
KATHERINE *is suddenly animated.*
KATHERINE. You know I think this Government's appalling. But on the other hand, let's face it, given what's going on, it's just stupid not to go and grab some dough for yourself.
MARION. It's more than stupid. It's irresponsible.
KATHERINE. I mean give it to the good guys that's my philosophy. If we don't make the money someone else will.
(*The Secret Rapture*, Faber & Faber, p. 41)

At the end of *Top Girls* Marlene engages in a furious row with Joyce. Presented in 1982 the scene shows great prescience on the part of Caryl Churchill:

MARLENE. . . . on on into the sunset. I think the eighties are going to be stupendous.
JOYCE. Who for?
MARLENE. For me. / I think I'm going up up up.
JOYCE. Oh for you. Yes, I'm sure they will.
MARLENE. And for the country, come to that. Get the economy back on its feet and whoosh. She's a tough lady, Maggie. I'd give her a job. / She just needs to hang in there. This country
JOYCE. You voted for them, did you?
MARLENE. needs to stop whining. / Monetarism is not stupid.
JOYCE. Drink your tea and shut up, pet.
MARLENE. It takes time, determination. No more slop. / And
JOYCE: Well I think they're filthy bastards.
(*Top Girls*, Methuen, pp. 83–4)

The character of Marlene's hapless daughter, Angie, depicts the no-hopers in Thatcher's Britain, and her lot was recognised by Harold Pinter, who felt stifled during this time:

I think there's a similar attitude in the US and England about how to treat the poor, the homeless, the disabled, which mainly is to ignore them.
(interview in 1988; Mel Gussow, *Conversations With Pinter*, Nick Hern Books, 1994, p. 68)

Howard Brenton was yet another playwright acutely depressed by the 1980s:

There was bound to be grief when Thatcherite free-market

> principles met the arts and cultural activity (the arts being both worthless and priceless).

According to Brenton,

> Some kind of evil was abroad in our society; a palpable degradation of the spirit. The experience of the eighties was of a philistine hurricane against the idea of culture itself.
> (Brenton, *Hot Irons*, Nick Hern Books, 1995, p. 73)

Brenton cites *Serious Money* and *Pravda* (Brenton and Hare) as reflecting amorality in the public world. Martin Amis's novel *Money* is a further indictment of the time. Its hero, John Self, is obsessed with money:

> Selina [his girlfriend] says I'm not capable of true love. It isn't true. I truly love money. Truly I do. Oh, money, I love you. You're so democratic: you've got no favourites. You even things out for me and my kind.
> (Amis, *Money*, Penguin Books, 1985, p. 238)

This overwhelming preoccupation with 'money' helps to contextualise Mrs Thatcher's suggestion, seriously offered, that nobody would have heard of the Good Samaritan if he hadn't been rich.

Dramatising the City: people at work

Serious Money is a dramatisation of London's financial institutions at work. It is, of course, more stylised and impressionistic than documentary in form but it does reflect the hurly-burly of share dealing, and it lets all the characters speak for themselves and describe their materialistic attitude to making money. In this respect the play presents both the appearance and reality of what is going on – something for which theatre is ideally suited.

In her 1982 play *Top Girls*, Churchill was brilliantly able to question feminist ambition by showing her young working women to be efficient, confident and successful (and, on stage, as likely as not, attractive). To all appearances they are admirable. However, when they speak to each other in the office they reveal a hard, insensitive, dismissive quality. The implication, coming from the stage, is to question whether replacing men in the workplace and aspiring to high position is a desirable aim if it means adopting masculine aggression and competitiveness. Similarly, *Serious Money* gives us a compelling, speedy, exciting world in the modern marketplace (where the women are as powerful and ruthless as the men), while at the same time questioning the values on display and the cost to those in the Third World who are cruelly exploited, and wholly disregarded when their produce reaches the market. For all its phenomenal wealth and glamour in the 1980s, the City comes steeped in scandal and corruption – a fact which the play does not ignore. We watch these people at work and are compelled to make a judgement.

Since the sixteenth century, dramatists in Europe and North America have exploited the fascination people have for watching other people at work. Plays treating this fall into various categories, but generally there is more than a purely naturalistic display of activity under scrutiny.

At one extreme the central character is partly defined in terms of his/her occupation. It is part of their identity: Ibsen's Solness (*The Master Builder*) is an architect, Miller's Willy Loman is, essentially, a salesman, Bill Maitland (in Osborne's *Inadmissible Evidence*) is a solicitor. At the other extreme the entire workplace, and much of the workforce, is reconstructed on stage (for example, Ben Jonson's *Bartholomew Fair*, Arnold Wesker's *The Kitchen* and *The Journalists*, Peter Nichols' *The National Health*, and David Storey's *The Contractor*). These are all plays with large casts, making heavy demands on production and design. However, employment is always dramatised with a purpose in these plays. Wesker, for example, has written:

> *The Kitchen* is not about cooking, it's about man and his relationship to work. *The Journalists* is not about journalism, it is about the poisonous human need to cut better men down to our size, from which need we all suffer in varying degrees.
> (Arnold Wesker, Penguin Plays, vol. IV, 1980, p. 9)

In *The Contractor*, as in Peter Whelan's *The Bright and Bold Design*, the aesthetic achievement of the work being done is very important and is considered. Men and women at work are staged expressionistically in Eugene O'Neill's *The Hairy Ape* and Sophie Treadwell's *Machinal* to show the dehumanising effect of repetitive physical labour.

Other dramatists have focused on how a community is trapped within an oppressive kind of employment by their natural environment, with consequences close to tragedy: D.H. Lawrence, J.M. Synge and Federico García Lorca present characters in conflict with, variously, the local coal mines, the sea and the land. Exploitation of workers has produced propaganda in drama, as in Odets' *Waiting for Lefty* or Sarah Daniels' *Gut Girls*, while David Mamet, in *Glengarry Glen Ross*, exposes the ruthless competitiveness of the estate agents in their office.

A whole sub-genre of plays, many very accomplished and successful, have followed Shakespeare and his presentation of the Mechanicals and their backstage rehearsals in *A Midsummer Night's Dream*. There is always good fun to be had at the expense of amateurs playing beyond their capacity, but several dramatists have found professional performers just as easy targets, for example, Arthur Wing Pinero in *Trelawny of the 'Wells'* (1898), Ronald Harwood in *The Dresser* (1980) and Michael Frayn in *Noises Off* (1982).

To portray the nature and purpose of the work being pursued is the dramatists' motive in all these plays, as it is in Churchill's *Serious Money*. The culture of high finance in the 1980s and the 'play world' created to define its working will be considered later but first it may be useful to summarise the factual details which were absorbed by the dramatist before turning them into a play.

The London Stock Exchange

The London Stock Exchange and the Bank of England, both situated in 'the City', constitute the centres of high finance in Britain. The Stock Exchange has steadily evolved for over two hundred years, during which time strong traditions of membership have been established and business practice has been constantly scrutinised and regulated to ensure the highest standards and behaviour in selling stocks and shares. Stocks and shares are the securities of a company, by the selling of which it raises capital. Buyers of stocks or debentures receive a fixed rate of interest in return for the loan they make to the firm. They are the creditors of the company and a firm's failure to pay their interest can result in its bankruptcy. Shareholders buy a stake or shares in a company and are the owners of the company, in proportion to their shareholding. They receive a dividend which will vary according to the firm's fluctuating profits. Larger accumulations of shares gives its holder greater voting power over company policy and the composition of the board of directors.

In 1986, immediately prior to the writing of *Serious Money*, the Exchange introduced the most revolutionary set of changes in living memory, quickly defined as 'Big Bang': the practice of share dealing was radically altered, and Churchill's play makes much of the ensuing explosive conflicts which affected everybody: relations between generations, professional colleagues and international financial centres.

> The London Stock Exchange is the organisation that provides the framework for buying and selling shares. It brings companies and investors together and provides rules to ensure the stock market works efficiently and fairly.
>
> Buying and selling shares takes place today either over the telephone or electronically through computer terminals. The Exchange continually monitors this trading to ensure it is conducted according to its rules.
>
> The London Stock Exchange provides markets for all types of companies, allowing them to raise capital to fund growth and to have their shares more widely traded.
>
> (*Share Ownership for All*, Stock Exchange, 1977)

The Exchange is vitally important in the national scene. Over ten million people own shares directly and many others are connected indirectly through business, pension or insurance schemes. It is not exclusively readers of the *Financial Times* who are affected by its workings.

The first joint stock company, where the public subscribed to shares, goes back to 1553 when 240 merchants in the City paid £25 each to fund an expeditionary fleet which sailed from Deptford in order to find a north-eastern passage to the Far East (China, in fact) for trading purposes. The fleet didn't reach China, but was well received in Russia by Czar Ivan who set up an advantageous trading agreement which, in turn, led to the creation of the Muscovy Company. This company, controlled by its shareholders, set the pattern for future joint stock companies, and the firm link between membership of the Stock Exchange and Freemen of the City (in effect, members of Livery Companies).

As companies grew in number so the profession of stockjobbing developed in London. Meeting, very noisily at first, in the Royal Exchange, by 1698 brokers were putting out a 'Daily Price List' (recording the fluctuating fortunes of companies – forerunner of the 'Daily Official List' of today) Certain coffee houses were also well-known meeting places (Jonathan's – which, in 1773, was named the first 'Stock Exchange' – and Garraway's) where they conducted business.

The establishment of the Bank of England during the reign of William III in 1694 began the practice of Government raising funds by the issue of stock (at first to fund the war with France, but later to contend with the national debt). Governments have subsequently raised funds through the issue of war loans and the sale of gilts (Government bonds).

Companies proliferated during the industrial revolution, notably in support of the thriving railway system, and this led to the development of regional stock exchanges throughout Britain. These were grouped into six in 1967, and eventually, in 1973, all the exchanges in the British Isles amalgamated to form the Stock Exchange of Great Britain and Ireland, by which time a 26-storey building had been opened in the City to accommodate it.

In 1979 the abolition of exchange controls forced London to compete with the other world finance centres, New York and Tokyo, which were altogether better placed to compete for foreign business; and when Thatcher's radical Conservative government was tracking down restrictive practices and monopolies in the 1980s, the London Stock Exchange was found wanting. A lengthy and expensive court case ensued from the discovery of 150 restrictive practices operating in the Exchange, but in 1986 a compromise deal was agreed between the Government and the Chairman of the Exchange leading to Big Bang, which introduced a number of fundamental changes to the rules and practices of the Stock Exchange..

Big Bang

These changes might be summarised as follows:

1 Rules of membership were changed. Member firms could be owned by a single outside corporation. Previously control had to be in the hands of individual members. A result was

that many firms were bought by UK and overseas banks or investment houses.

2 Voting rights in the Exchange were transferred to member firms instead of residing with individual members.
3 Minimum scales of commission were abolished. Members became free to negotiate charges with their clients.
4 The separation of member firms into brokers and jobbers was to end (this had been formalised in 1908). All firms now became brokers/dealers able to represent clients in the market, or principals, buying and selling shares on their own acccount.
5 A computer-based quotation system was introduced: Stock Exchange Automated Quotations (SEAQ) which displays prices and bids of over 2,000 securities on screens for the benefit of brokers and dealers. Dealing takes place on telephones or through computer systems.
6 Following the Financial Services Act 1986, a new system of self-regulation to ensure standards was introduced.

The reputation of the City

The development of international dealing in the new technological age, and the vast sums of money being transacted, have posed temptations for the unscrupulous which could not be resisted, and in the last decades of the twentieth century the reputation of the City has been dented. The longstanding loyalties associated with well-established firms and the wholehearted acceptance of the motto of the Exchange – 'My word is my bond' are questioned in *Serious Money*, but the play was not the first statement of condemnation. The Labour MP Denis MacShane is recorded as saying: 'Winston Churchill, in 1927, described the gentlemen of the City as "the glittering scum which floats upon the deep river of production". There has been something very 1920s about the 1990s.'

Will Hutton, in his economic analysis, *The State We're In* (Vintage, 1996) – an explanation of Britain's economic decline towards the end of the century – was not impressed by the City:

> Public institutions are not the only victims of the new corruption. The City of London has become a byword for speculation, inefficiency and cheating. Given the power to regulate their own affairs, City financial markets and institutions have conspicuously

> failed to meet any reasonable standard of honest dealing with the public or their own kind. (p.5)

And David Lascelles, writing about the unprecedented spate of City scandals as well as company takeovers in Britain and the United States in the 1980s, names Boesky, Guinness and Collyer for insider dealing, share price manipulation and fraud.

The behaviour of the characters in *Serious Money* should not be regarded as fantastic. It is firmly based on the evidence of contemporary events (with a little dramatic licence where actual murder is concerned).

Playwright and theatre

In his review in *The Times*, the critic Irving Wardle not only sums up the play astutely but also recognises its place in the Royal Court tradition:

> Caryl Churchill's post Big-Bang 'city comedy' is a piece in the great Royal Court tradition: an angry, witty, front-line report on Britain, introducing characters and environments new to the theatre that affect all our lives. It is also staged and cast with high-gloss precision.

The same could have been said of *Top Girls* in 1982, with the same director and at the same theatre. The reviewers of that production praised the quality of the seven actresses who played sixteen different women drawn from historical and modern times, representing different ages and social backgrounds. The play is a passionate assertion of the rights of women in the face of centuries of mistreatment.

The Royal Court Theatre, in Sloane Square, London, home of the English Stage Company, has been the leading theatre of new writing in Britain since the mid-1950s when the early work of Osborne, Wesker and Arden ushered in a renaissance for British drama which continued through the century. Most of the contemporary dramatists whose plays fill the shelves of today's bookshops have been staged first at the Royal Court, which speaks highly of the theatre's ability to identify good modern drama and their commitment to supporting it.

Never was this commitment more publicly or profoundly demonstrated than during the 1960s when the theatre defied the

Office of the Lord Chamberlain to such an extent that it brought about the closure of the Office and the effective end of theatre censorship, which had operated in Britain since 1737. In particular their support of John Osborne and Edward Bond, two of their most important playwrights, was overwhelming. The theatre even turned itself into a private club to circumvent the Lord Chamberlain's Office and allow their plays to be performed.

A loyal audience has come to expect radical subjects, relevant to the times, dealt with passionately and seriously. Some plays have positively shocked audiences (as did Bond's *Saved* as long ago as 1965), causing some revision of the function of theatre: Bond's plays are rarely diverting entertainments. But the Royal Court audience has preferred to be provoked rather than patronised. 'The form and pressure of the times' is still a priority, and 'the state of England' remains the essential subject. The theatre has been committed to challenging subjects, both national and international, and in recent years plays have dealt with Northern Ireland, inner city deprivation (in Britain and the USA), the disaffected young, mental health, sexual, national, and international politics. Recent initiatives have seen the close relationship with Joseph Papp's New York theatre expand to a collaboration with dramatists from Uganda and Palestine. Whatever challenge may have come from the Royal National Theatre, the Royal Shakespeare Company or elsewhere, the Royal Court, by general consent, remains the most significant theatre for new and progressive writing in Britain.

Caryl Churchill is well established as one of Britain's foremost playwrights, with a very impressive catalogue of plays to her name (see the chronology on pp. v–viii). Many of these plays were first performed at the Royal Court, where she was resident dramatist from 1974–5. And many of her plays were directed by Max Stafford-Clark. At one time the artistic director of the theatre (and of the Joint Stock Theatre Company with which Churchill has worked, employing their method of workshopping productions in the early stages), Stafford-Clark is well placed to appreciate Churchill's distinctive quality as a dramatist. In his words, 'She has an incisiveness, a political astuteness and an ability to analyse, together with a theatrical inventiveness that is always exciting.'

The socialist and feminist sympathies evident in her work are very clear (she has also worked with the feminist group

Monstrous Regiment), and she figures prominently in books on these subjects. But it would be unwise to label her in any way that might limit or restrict her subject matter; she is always re-creating her dramaturgy and as she states,

> If someone says 'a socialist playwright' or 'a feminist playwright' that can suggest to some people something rather narrow which doesn't cover as many things as you might be thinking about.

The stimulating practical challenge of her plays is probably another major reason why Churchill became extremely popular with students in the 1980s and 1990s, displacing Pinter and Beckett in production exercises. *Cloud Nine, Top Girls, Fen* and *Serious Money* have become modern classics and are regularly staged.

Her contemporaries are also fulsome in their appreciation. David Hare is unstinting in his praise of the density of effort and imagination that he sees in all her work:

> Caryl's politics I'm sure are completely different from my own. But you can't not know that Caryl is serious. She's fantastically talented: everything she writes is very, very interesting. She's just the real thing. You don't go saying, 'Ooh, I hope they toe the line. Ooh, I hope they say something I agree with.' Caryl's a great mind, so you go to find out what Caryl's thinking now. And it's exciting to find out what Caryl's thinking about.
> ('An interview with David Hare', p. 17, in Hersh Zeifman (ed.) *David Hare: A Casebook*, Garland Publishing, 1994)

A 'city comedy'?

The choice of generic title is a clear guide as to how we should respond to *Serious Money*, because the first 'city comedies' of the early seventeenth century were satiric in tone and purpose. Jonson, Marston and Middleton made the contemporary citizens of London the subject of their wit and scorn in a new kind of play. At a time of social aspiration and material ambition a new attitude of self-interest and individualism was clearly discernible. Middleton, in particular, has been identified as one of the first to explore the bourgeois mentality. Although comedy and wit were included in these city comedies they were notably lacking in the warmth and goodwill which underpinned such earlier studies of

London merchants as *The Shoemaker's Holiday* by Dekker, where relations between family members, between the sexes and between citizens and figures of authority were fundamentally acceptable, optimistic and socially worthwhile.

Nevertheless, the contemporary life of the city was the subject and the city was always London. Caryl Churchill has limited the world of her play to people who work in and around the City financial institutions (including some from abroad) immediately after Big Bang. Many of the first reviewers stated, unequivocally, that the play was 'very funny', but the humour is barbed, satiric and always highlights the anti-social or self-obsessed attitudes of the characters. Some confusion results from this combination: an empathy with the energy and commitment shown by dealers, and a questioning of their values. The world is both attractive and dangerous. How are we expected to respond to this ambivalence? Critics have found the play confusing in other ways as well. What exactly has Jake Todd done? And what exactly has happened to him? We never know. We are not as interested in him as Scilla naturally is – until it turns out that what she really wants to uncover is not the cause of his death but the whereabouts of his money, or at least 'her share'.

The most disturbing aspect of the play is the lack of a moral or emotional through-line. No character provides a standard by which to judge the others. This works as satire, however, because the whole play-world is shown to be corrupt, and is left essentially unchanged at the end. To feel that you are part of this money-making world, that you can be hugely avaricious and not feel guilty, and that the Devil really does have the best tunes, can be exhilarating for both actors and audience. Critics have often attested to the excitement generated by the high-octane acting that the play has produced.

A direct keynote to the style of the play is provided by the publicity which accompanied the production. Posters, programme and text featured a cartoon by Gerald Scarfe illustrating 'The Financier'. What might be regarded as 'funny – a comic portrait even' might also be considered obscenely nasty. The Financier is a grotesque personification of Greed, an obese figure made up of currency notes (pounds and dollars), vomiting a mass of currency from his fat jowls. It sets the tone for a largely damning exposure of greed in the City, more pervasive than in seventeenth-century city comedy. All relationships in the play –

personal or business – are based on self-interest. Personal acquisition is the all-pervading drive, for, as the play makes clear, 'Sexy greedy *is* the late eighties' (p. 92). Satire is a more appropriate response than comedy to this moral delinquency.

In Churchill's *Top Girls* the successful office executive, Nell, acknowledges her selling skills, and is presented with similar qualities by her client, Shona. She knows that employers have qualms about them being women:

> NELL. They think we listen to the buyer's doubts. They think we consider his needs and his feelings.
> SHONA. I never consider people's feelings.
> NELL. I was selling for six years, I can sell anything, I've sold in three continents, and I'm jolly as they come but I'm not very nice.
> SHONA. I'm not very nice. (p. 61)

These uncomfortable admissions pale beside the confessions in *Serious Money*. For example, note Scilla's claim:

> I'm greedy and completely amoral.
> I've the cunning and connections of the middle class
> And I'm tough as a yob. (p. 110)

This is, at least, honest: but all the more shocking for that. It applies to her brother as well. As Jacinta says, 'Don't be embarassed, Jake, you're young and greedy, I like to see it.' Most of the big operators use Jake for inside information so there is no reason why he should immediately suspect his father's old friend Frosby of informing on him to the authorities.

Dramatic structure

The scenic structure of *Serious Money* is Elizabethan and as with the plays of Shakespeare and his contemporaries what is needed for performance is an open, flexible stage with numerous entrances and exits. Nothing too elaborate. Every scene opens with a change of character, often in a new location, and these are soon identified. The seventeen named characters have sometimes required doubling or trebling by the actors but this need not lead to difficulties of identification because their names are constantly being mentioned, and they frequently announce themselves, as Zackerman does:

> So cut the nostalgia. I'm the guy they're talking about, Zac.
> I'm here for my bank . . . (p. 12)

And Duckett:

> I'm Duckett. I enjoy the *Financial Times*.
> It's fun reading about other people's crimes. (p. 31)

In the original production there was a strong visual statement on stage (designed by Peter Hartwell) with the bare central acting space surrounded by walls which were filled with banks of television screens, telephones, and bottles of champagne – signifying the working environment of the City dealers, and used for all the dealing scenes. Any scenes away from the City are easily defined, and are often introduced verbally, so we know where we are. For example, 'TK *on machine*: Hello, this is the office of Marylou Baines' (p. 22), or Corman holding a meeting: 'So what's on the agenda today?' (p. 31). Jacinta Condor, *flying first class* at the beginning of Act Two, can be introduced on stage by light, sitting in an appropriate seat. For a play that embraces incalculable wealth, the staging requires no frills. The play relies on acting.

Two other structural devices are important. One is the use of telephones, and much information is passed quickly between characters on the phone; the other is the use of flashbacks when characters are seen talking in the past. Zac Zackerman has an important narrative role, chorus-like, introducing many of these scenes, as does Scilla.

The play is prefaced with a scene from Thomas Shadwell's 1692 play *The Volunteers, or The Stockjobbers*. As in many of her plays, Caryl Churchill provides an historical context for a modern work. Here the essential point is made: 'no matter whether it turns to use or not; the main end verily is to turn the penny in the way of stock jobbing, that's all.' Stocks and shares have always meant profit in some direction.

The early scenes of *Serious Money* form an exposition, communicating the international scale of the financial world (Sweden, Japan, Belgium, New York, Hong Kong, Frankfurt are some of the places mentioned in the early scenes), and the characters and family associated with Scilla. Thereafter the play follows two 'plots', which connect the key characters. One concerns the death of Jake Todd and Scilla's search for the guilty party among his business associates – a plot that is never quite tied up; the other concerns Billy Corman's attempt to take over the Albion Company by getting a 'war party' of business colleagues to buy up shares secretly. Corman's use of industrial spies, his discovery of the inefficiency of the symbolically named 'Albion', together with his plans to 'rationalise' the company and render it efficient, give the whole takeover a metaphorical dimension, applicable to Britain generally. The personnel in these plots can be more closely considered when examining the play's treatment of characterisation.

Characterisation

A vital feature of any play, and one of the first things to be faced by the actors and director, is the dramatist's approach to characterisation. Is psychological development of character and the psychological interplay of relationships a priority, or are characters serving a more thematic function in the grand design of the play? Both dimensions may well be involved, but initially an actor would approach a character in a Harold Pinter or a Tennessee Williams play rather differently from one in Beckett or Brecht.

There is a strong tradition in comedy of treating characters two dimensionally, and satire, as a form, usually highlights a particular aberration in a character. Some plays make use of 'conventional' characters (you will regularly find in Elizabethan/Jacobean drama court clowns/fools or satirical malcontents, for example). And some plays draw their characters from the morality tradition and give them a symbolic or allegorical dimension (as in Tourneur's *The Revenger's Tragedy*). In *Serious Money* actors have to deal with 'character types' for the most part. It is quickly understood that all the characters in the play are money-mad, but Caryl Churchill does not distinguish between them on the basis of individual or moral failings. Rather, the characters are mostly defined by their profession, as given in the cast-list, and distinguished by their patterns of speech. So, in a number of cases, actors have to play out these set roles (such as chairman, corporate raider, businesswoman, dealer, etc). It is indicative that Duckett, chairman of Albion, and Ms Biddulph, a white knight, are 'both from the north' which helps to place them in the tradition of northern industrialists – character types known in Britain as much from theatre convention as social fact.

The actors, however, have a particular challenge in this play. Because there are seventeen named characters, and few theatres can afford that many actors, most actors have to play more than one role, and every role must be distinct in performance. This is where 'technique' is demanded. It is essential that the company show that they are in the same play, and that they understand the style that is being adopted. It is equally important that when they start speaking on stage they immediately project the character they are representing at that moment. Each character is distinctive, so the actors must know what their employment is, what their ambitions are, and how they speak – in conventional Stanislavskian mode. Each, in turn, will then stand out against the panorama of the company on stage. It may be necessary to adopt a company policy towards the verse rhyme in the language. A sing-song delivery or heavy emphasis on the last syllable of the line could become very annoying for the audience. Language is nevertheless a key defining element for each character.

The majority of characters are brokers, dealers or jobbers and they tend to be used not only to forward one plot or the other but also to describe the effects of Big Bang on the two generations who make up the modern City.

Scilla, Jake and Grimes are a contrasting trio who represent the new generation of City trader, and between them a new and distinctive culture, based on confident self-assertion, is shown at work. They know how big money works, and how to get it, and they don't go unnoticed. Part of Zac Zackerman's role in the play is to keep the audience informed about the other characters. An American banker living in England, he is a reliable, well-informed witness and a valuable source of information on other characters and the contemporary financial world:

ZAC.
The financial world won't be the same again
Because the traders are coming down the fast lane . . .
If you're making the firm ten million you want a piece of the action . . .
Guy over forty's got any sense he takes his golden handshake

and goes.
Because the new guys are hungrier and hornier . . .
It's like Darwin says, survival of the fit,
Now here in England, it's just beginning to hit. (p. 15)

We see the three – Scilla, Jake and Grimes – at work in their dealing rooms early in the play (when some character features are shown) but it is in the next scene when they are talking and drinking in the Liffe champagne bar that they openly declare their priorities. The scene could be quoted in full because it is so compact and revealing about all three characters – providing vital information for actors. Grimes is greedy and aggressive, Scilla is greedy and ambitious, and Jake is greedy and calculating ('I've no intention of working after I'm thirty'). From the start they are seen talking of salaries in millions, and they have absolutely no respect for the older generation, the holders of traditional stock-exchange values, here represented by Greville Todd (father of Jake and Scilla), a stockbroker, and Frosby, a jobber.

Greville is a constant source of annoyance and frustration to his daughter Scylla, who considers him inept and embarrassing. Frosby laments the passing of the old, pre-Big Bang stockmarket in terms that are nostalgic and sentimental:

The stock exchange was a village street.
You strolled about and met your friends.
Now we never seem to meet.
I don't get asked much at weekends . . .

Since Big Bang the floor is bare,
They deal in offices on screens.
But if the chap's not really there
You can't be certain what he means. (p. 20)

He has been made redundant ('The firm's not doing awfully well') and is full of resentment towards Greville and his family, to the extent that he is prepared to 'let the DTI investigate' Jake. Now that 'the City's not mine any more . . . let it fall'. He openly admits that in the present climate 'I'm very frightened' – a rare moment of honest insecurity in the play.

Pen portraits of other characters are provided in Jake's diary – read by Greville to Scilla – essential information for the actors involved:

GREVILLE.
Marylou Baines
Was originally a poor girl from the plains.
She set out to make whatever she wanted hers
And now she's one of America's top arbitrageurs
(second only to Boesky).
SCILLA
Condor, Jacinta.
GREVILLE.
A very smart lady from South America who comes here every
winter.
Europe sends aid, her family says thanks
And buys Eurobonds in Swiss banks.
SCILLA.
Corman.
GREVILLE.
Billy Corman,
William the Conqueror, the great invader,
A very successful dawn raider. (p. 27)

By the time Zac introduces Corman's plot to take over Albion, all these characters are established.

Language

The most striking feature of the language of *Serious Money* is the use of rhyming couplets, because the use of verse is so rare in modern English drama. Rhyming couplets are often associated with comedy, and critics tend to describe the verse in Churchill's play as doggerel, derived from nineteenth-century pantomine. Although it would be an exaggeration to say that the language is poetic, the verse does serve a number of dramatic purposes. Firstly, it is fun, and always under a witty control. The idea of verse apparently provided a stimulus and breakthrough for the writer when she was weighed down with documentary material after a lot of research. It was then soon clear to her that 'it does have the effect of driving the play incredibly fast, which seems very right for it.' The verse gives the language a distinct energy. Often the lines end with words of two or three syllables, with an internal rhyme that is pleasing to have brought off – assiduity/ ingenuity, a failure/Australia, our position/acquisition, institution/ contribution, where none of the rhymes are as blatant and provocative as Corman's,

> I spent a good weekend once in Caracas.
> You don't by any chance play the maracas?'

Jacinta uses a number of comic verse patterns, for example:

> If I buy or sell
> I always do well
> So don't worry about it, my pet.
> Whatever I get
> I look after you
> And Corman will too
> I expect. (p. 67)

The verse form has the further consequence of passing comment on the characters of the play. In the city comedies of Ben Jonson poetry allows characters give expression to vast imaginative excesses. They are selfish and exploitative but the poetry makes them at times truly larger than life. The characters in Churchill's play, however, come across as uniformly shallow, which could very well be her conclusion on the consequence of their single-minded obsession with money, and rhyme occasionally helps to expose the banality of thought being expressed.

Even sex is distorted in this world, continuously reduced in status by the proliferation of obscenities, and the sexist attitudes of the male dealers who don't discriminate at all between the young women in the workplace. The ultimate perversion is ironically underlined when Zac and Jacinta declare their mutual attraction in terms of business, and look forward to a good sleep. The rhyming here, not very subtle, serves only to reduce the quality of the personal relationship.

> JACINTA.
> I can't do bad business just because I feel romantic.
> ZAC.
> The way you do business, Jacinta, drives me completely frantic.
> JACINTA.
> I love the way you are so obsessed when you're thinking about your bids.
> ZAC.
> I love that terrible hospital scam / and the drug addicted kids . . .
>
> JACINTA.
> Zac, you're so charming, I'm almost as fond

Of you as I am of a eurobond.
ZAC.
I thought we'd never manage to make a date.
You're more of a thrill than a changing interest rate.
JACINTA.
This is a very public place to meet.
ZAC.
Maybe we ought to go up to your suite.
They get up to go.
ZAC.
Did you ever play with a hoop when you were a child and when it stops turning it falls down flat?
I feel kind of like that.
JACINTA.
I am very happy. My feeling for you is deep.
But will you mind very much if we go to sleep? (p. 105)

There are also a number of exchanges in the play, almost knockabout in mood, where rhyme adds to the rhythm.

The play, however, uses some other stylistic devices which need to be considered. Several characters have lengthy set speeches of exposition either in prose or in non-comic verse. In fact most of the main characters hold centre stage at some point, stating very clearly their concerns, their business, or their intentions. We hear from Greville, Zac, Frosby, Corman, Jake, Marylou, Scilla, Jacinta and finally, Gleason. In a cumulative build-up and with Nigel Ajibala, they appear to be interconnected in a series of spurious financial deals on an international scale and most of them have cause to be concerned by any scandal involving Jake – it might easily reach as far as them. Their set speeches are always focused on the financial context, so Jake's flight of imagination is all the more marked when he is talking to Zac about the British obsession with land.

JAKE
Tell you something. I fancy the ocean.
Instead of land. I'd like to own a big cube of sea, right down to the bottom, all the fish, weeds, the lot.
There'd be takers for that.
ZAC.
Sure, it's a great notion.

JAKE.
Or air. Space. A square metre going straight up into infinity.
ZAC.
And a section of God at the top. (pp. 36–7)

One commentator has argued that it explains Jake's suicide – he simply can live no longer in the finance-obsessed world.

Caryl Churchill also employs her technique of overlapping dialogue – used in earlier plays. The four types of overlapping are explained in the Note on Layout immediately before the play. The effect of this is twofold: it adds a surface naturalism where a number of people are talking at the same time, and it makes the audience concentrate more carefully on the performance.

Another distinctive feature of language in this play is the use of financial jargon in the dealing scenes. Churchill uses this very skilfully. For example, the play begins with activity in '*three different dealing rooms simultaneously*': the effect is strongly impressionistic and conveys a day's business across a variety of dealing situations. Gilts, futures and foreign bonds are all being dealt simultaneously, while the scenes also show a level of individual greed and high living on the part of the characters. This is the City at work. Churchill orchestrates the dealing terminology to give the effect of frantic activity. We don't even know what precise contracts, products or commodities are being offered for sale. Nor does it in fact matter. However, the trading scene is carefully constructed and the text is timed to intersect and to explode in the 'Futures Song' at the end.

Critical responses to *Serious Money*

The enthusiastic response of Irving Wardle, theatre critic of *The Times*, to *Serious Money* has already been noted. He welcomed unreservedly the originality of subject matter, seriousness of purpose and quality of performance. As with all Caryl Churchill's new plays, *Serious Money* attracted wide critical attention both when it opened at the Royal Court Theatre and when it transferred to Wyndham's Theatre in the West End, where a larger stage suited the play very well. The critical response was generally favourable, but not always without reservation. Questions were raised about the plot, the use of verse, and the complexity of the information relating to the personnel and the business of the City.

Many critics described the play as 'brilliant', referring to the dramatist's grasp of her material, and Michael Ratcliffe in the *Observer* recognised 'the real thing: theatre of language, movement, energy, purpose and wit'. Otherwise, critics responded variously. For example, Jim Hiley described the play as 'superbly informative, supremely intelligent' (*The Listener*), whereas Steve Grant found the script 'frankly incomprehensible' (*Time Out*), and Hiley, while describing the plot involving Jake's death as 'wonderful' also admitted that 'it fizzles out with a tantalisingly off-hand reference to MI5 and the CIA'. Martin Hoyle pinpointed the problem of the esoteric material: 'Insiders may well enjoy the play. Outsiders may experience a numbing boredom' (*Financial Times*). Insiders certainly did enjoy the play and there are many references to the groups of city workers who attended and responded gleefully to seeing their kind on stage. Max Stafford-Clark has explained this peculiar phenomenon:

> If you capture accurately enough the world of the people you are depicting, then it's very flattering and they will come and see it, just as people did in the Restoration.
> (*Vanity Fair*, December 1987)

Stafford-Clark's direction was universally praised. The energy of the company, notably in ensemble scenes – dealing scenes, the scene of the hunt, and especially in the rousing songs which end each Act – was exhilarating.

Perhaps the most controversial feature of the play was the language, and the use of rhyming verse. Michael Ratcliffe considered this to be a great drawback: 'Where iambics are used, the scansion is erratic and annoying. And the rhyming of four-letter crudities becomes predictable and uninventive. The idea is to catch the desperate furore and noisiness of the dealers' world, but the text needs much more highlighting and pointing . . . the overlapping dialogue passages are just messy' (*Observer*). Such strictures were refuted by other reviewers. Amelia Howe Kritzer, for example, found the language perfectly acceptable: 'The driving rhythm of the verse serves quite effectively to convey the frenetic pace at which life in the City moves, and its restraints suggest the extent to which the supposedly powerful barons of high finance are controlled by the environment in which they operate' (*Theatre Journal* XXXIV, 3 October 1987).

The play's lasting quality is assured by the mature satirical stance of the dramatist. This is not merely a topical swipe at Yuppie fashion (as some foreign reviewers claimed). There is no suggestion that the new breed of City dealers are any worse than their predecessors:

GRIMES.
We're only doing just the same
All you bastards always done.
New Faces in your old square mile,
Making money with a smile,
Just as clever, just as vile. (p. 88)

As Michael Billington recognised, the play 'attacks the City's greed and fear with zest rather than self-righteousness' (*Guardian*). *Serious Money* is indeed topical, showing aspects of Britain immediately after Big Bang and the Guinness scandal; it contributes distinctively to the political theatre of the 1980s, making its own telling judgement on the ethics of Thatcherism. But it also remains fresh, and it has a continuing relevance as a satire on greed and the ruthless workings of a financial centre.

Further Reading

Plays by Caryl Churchill

Plays: One, London: Methuen, 1985 (*Owners, Traps, Vinegar Tom, Light Shining in Buckinghamshire, Cloud Nine*)
Plays: Two, London: Methuen, 1990 (*Softcops, Top Girls, Fen, Serious Money*)
Plays: Three, London: Nick Hern Books, 1998 (*Ice Cream, Mad Forest, Thyestes, The Skriker, Lives of the Great Poisoners, A Mouthful of Birds*)
Objections to Sex and Violence, published in *Plays by Women, Volume 4*, London: Methuen, 1985
Shorts, London: Nick Hern Books, 1990 (short plays)

Writing about Churchill

A most useful companion is Linda Fitzsimmons' *File on Churchill* (London: Methuen, 1989), which contains critical reactions to productions of her work, comments of the playwright, and a good bibliography including the many articles written on Churchill. Geraldine Cousin studies Churchill's development in *Churchill: The Playwright* (London: Methuen, 1989), and Phyllis Randall has edited *Caryl Churchill: A Casebook* (New York: Garland, 1988).

The following are among the more significant articles on *Serious Money*:

Laura L. Doan, 'Sexy Greedy is the Late Eighties: Power Systems in Amis's *Money* and Churchill's *Serious Money*', *The Minnesota Review* 34–5 (1990), pp. 69–80
Kimball King, '*Serious Money*: A Market Correction?' in *Caryl Churchill: A Casebook*, ed. Phyllis Randall (New York: Garland, 1988), pp. 151–60
Klaus Peter Müller, 'A Serious City Comedy: Fe-/Male History and Value Judgements in Caryl Churchill's *Serious Money*', *Modern Drama* 33 (1995), pp. 347–62

Judith Bayley Slagle, 'Shadwell's Volunteers through the Centuries: Power Structures Adapted in Scott's *Peveril of the Peak* and Churchill's *Serious Money*', *Restoration* 20.2 (1996), pp. 236–46

The following books, covering aspects of contemporary British drama, include sections on Churchill:

Sue-Ellen Case, *Feminism and Theatre*, London: Macmillan, 1988
Colin Chambers and Mike Prior, *Playwright's Progress: Patterns of Postwar British Drama*, Oxford: Amber Lane Press, 1987
Catherine Itzin, *Stages in The Revolution: Political Theatre in Britain since 1968*, London: Eyre Methuen, 1980
Leslie Ferris, *Acting Women: Images of Women in Theatre*, London: Macmillan, 1990
Helene Keyssar, *Feminist Theatre*, Basingstoke and London: Macmillan, 1984
C. W. E. Bigsby (ed.), *Contemporary English Drama: Stratford-upon-Avon Studies 19*, London: Edward Arnold, 1981
Michelene Wandor, *Carry on, Understudies: Theatre and Sexual Politics*, London: Routledge and Kegan Paul, 1986
Michelene Wandor, *Look Back in Gender: Sexuality and the Family in Post-War British Drama*, London: Methuen, 1987

Two books providing useful background to the period are:

Will Hutton, *The State We're In*, London: Vintage, 1996
Keith Peacock, *Thatcher's Theatre*, London: Greenwood, 1999

Serious Money

PREFACE

Serious Money takes place at the time of Big Bang, the deregulation of the City in 1986, when the markets were opened to foreign banks and the distinction between jobbers (who had shares available) and brokers (who bought and sold shares on their clients' behalf) was abolished. The men who had done these traditional jobs risked being replaced by young marketmakers whose companies could both own the stock and buy and sell it for clients. 'The financial world won't be the same again, Because the traders are coming down the fast lane,' explains Zac, an American setting up a trading branch of his bank, Klein Merrick, in London. Within a few weeks of Big Bang the Stock Exchange hardly existed in its previous form.

The play was written because Max Stafford-Clark asked me to take part in a two week workshop about the City at the Royal Court in September 1986. We had two weeks research, visiting Liffe, the Stock Exchange, the Metal Exchange, and so on, talking to people who worked in the City, and also to someone from War on Want who explained some of the consequences of international financial practices for the third world. Max had been interested in doing a play about the City for some time so it was a fortunate coincidence that Big Bang took place just after the workshop ended and that we were looking at the City at a moment of change and conflict.

After the workshop I went on learning more, about takeovers, about debt, about the scandals that kept the City in the news – Guinness, Boesky, Halpern. For weeks I was buried in cuttings from the Financial Times and only finally got a purchase on the material when I decided to write the play in verse.

To pick up *Serious Money* and have it fall open at a dealing scene might be daunting. But there's no need to grasp the details of the figures flying past to understand the plot, which is about an attempted takeover and a mysterious death.

Caryl Churchill, 1990

Serious Money was first performed at the Royal Court Theatre, London, on 21 March 1987, with the following cast:

SCILLA TODD, *a LIFFE dealer*	Lesley Manville
JAKE TODD, *Scilla's brother, a commercial paper dealer*	Julian Wadham
GRIMES, *a gilts dealer*	Gary Oldman
ZACKERMAN, *a banker with Klein Merrick*	Alfred Molina
MERRISON, *a banker, co-chief executive of Klein Merrick*	Burt Caesar
DURKFELD, *a trader, co-chief executive of Klein Merrick*	Allan Corduner
GREVILLE TODD, *Jake and Scilla's father, a stockbroker*	Allan Corduner
FROSBY, *a jobber*	Julian Wadham
T.K., *personal assistant*	Burt Caesar
MARYLOU BAINES, *an American arbitrageur*	Linda Bassett
JACINTA CONDOR, *a Peruvian businesswoman*	Meera Syal
NIGEL ABJIBALA, *an importer from Ghana*	Burt Caesar
BILLY CORMAN, *a corporate raider*	Gary Oldman
MRS ETHERINGTON, *a stockbroker*	Linda Bassett
DUCKETT, *chairman of Albion*	Allan Corduner
MS BIDDULPH, *a white knight*	Lesley Manville
DOLCIE STARR, *a PR consultant*	Linda Bassett
GREVETT, *a DTI inspector*	Julian Wadham
SOAT, *president of Missouri Gumballs*	Allan Corduner
GLEASON, *a Cabinet Minister*	Allan Corduner

Other parts played by the Company and members of the Royal Court Young Peoples' Theatre

Director	Max Stafford-Clark
Designer	Peter Hartwell
Lighting designer	Rick Fisher
Sound designer	Christopher Shutt
Musical director and arranger	Colin Sell
Keyboards	Colin Sell
Assistant director	Bo Barton
Stage manager	Bo Barton

Futures Song: words by Ian Dury, music by Micky Gallagher
Freedom Song: words by Ian Dury, music by Chaz Jankel

The play includes a scene from *The Volunteers, or The Stockjobbers* by Thomas Shadwell, 1692

Note on layout

A speech usually follows the one immediately before it BUT:

1: When one character starts speaking before the other has finished, the point of interruption is marked / .

eg. SCILLA: Leave the country. / Are you serious?
JAKE. They've taken my passport.

2: A character sometimes continues speaking right through another's speech:

eg. JAKE: No, it's just . . . I'm in a spot of bother with the authorities/but it's no problem, I'm sorting it
SCILLA: What have you done?
JAKE: out, it's more what the sorting might lead to

3: Sometimes a speech follows on from a speech earlier than the one immediately before it, and continuity is marked*.

eg. BRIAN: How much would it cost to shoot her through the head?*
TERRY: You can't get rid of your money in Crete.
Hire every speedboat, drink till you pass out, eat
Till you puke and you're still loaded with drachs.
MARTIN: }
DAVE: } Drach attack! drach attack!
VINCE: Why's a clitoris like a filofax?
DAVE and OTHERS: Every cunt's got one.
BRIAN: *And he says five grand.

where 'shoot her through the head?' is the cue to 'You can't get rid' and 'And he says five grand.'

4: Superior numerals appear where several conversations overlap at the same time.

eg. DAVE: I've got a certain winner for the 3.30 if anyone's interested.[4]
BRIAN: You haven't paid us yesterday's winnings yet.
DAVE: Leave it out, Brian, I always pay you.
KATHY: [4]Come on gilts. 2 at 4 the gilts.

where Kathy starts speaking as Dave finishes his first speech, but Brian and Dave continue their dialogue at the same time.

ACT ONE

A scene from The Volunteers, or The Stockjobbers *by Thomas Shadwell.*

HACKWELL, MRS HACKWELL, *and two jobbers.*

HACKWELL.

Well, have ye been enquiring? What Patents are they soliciting for, and what Stocks to dispose of?

FIRST JOBBER.

Why in truth there is one thing liketh me well, it will go all over England.

MRS HACKWELL.

What's that, I am resolved to be in it Husband.

FIRST JOBBER.

Why it is a Mouse-Trap, that will invite all mice in, nay rats too, whether they will or no: a whole share before the Patent is fifteen pound; after the Patent they will not take sixty: there is no family in England will be without 'em.

SECOND JOBBER.

I take it to be great Undertaking: but there is a Patent likewise on foot for one walking under Water, a share twenty pound.

MRS HACKWELL.

That would have been of great use to carry messages under the ice this last frost, before it would bear.

HACKWELL.

Look thee Lamb, between us, it's no matter whether it turns to use or not; the main end verily is to turn the penny in the way of stock jobbing, that's all.

FIRST JOBBER.

There is likewise one who will undertake to kill all fleas in all the families in England –

SECOND JOBBER.

There is likewise a Patent moved for, of bringing some Chinese Rope-Dancers over, the most exquisite in the world; considerable men have shares in it.

FIRST JOBBER.
But verily I question whether this be lawful or not?

HACKWELL.
Look thee, brother, if it be to a good end and that we ourselves have no share in the vanity or wicked diversion thereof by beholding of it but only use it whereby we may turn the penny, always considered that it is like to take and the said Shares will sell well; and then we shall not care whether the aforesaid dancers come over or no.

SECOND JOBBER.
There is another Patent in agitation for flying; a great virtuoso undertakes to outfly any post horse five mile an hour, very good for expresses and intelligence.

MRS HACKWELL.
May one have a share in him too?

SECOND JOBBER.
Thou mayst.

HACKWELL.
Look ye Brethren, hye ye into the city and learn what ye can; we are to have a Consultation at my house at four, to settle matters as to lowing and heightening of Shares: Lamb, let's away, we shall be too late.

Three different dealing rooms simultaneously. All have screens and phones.

Shares – GREVILLE
Gilts – GRIMES *and* OTHERS
Paper – JAKE *and* OTHERS

Shares

GREVILLE (*on phone*)
It's quite a large placement and what we've done is taken them onto our own books, one of the first deals of this kind we've done since Big Bang, yes . . . It's Unicorn Hotels, whom of course you know, they've acquired a chain of hotels in Belgium, and the main thing is they're a perfect mirror of their hotels here, 70 per cent business, 3 and 4 star. They acquired them for sixteen million, the assets are in fact valued at eleven million but that's historic and they're quite happy about that. The key to the deal is there's considerable earnings enhancement. It was a private owner who got into trouble, not bankrupt but a considerable squeeze on his assets, and they were able to get them cheap. I can offer you a million

shares, they're 63 to 4 in the market, I can let you have them for 62½ net. At the moment the profits are fourteen million pretax which is eleven million, the shares pay 4.14 with a multiple of 13.3. With the new hotels we expect to see a profit of twenty million next year paying 5.03 with the multiple falling to 12, so it's very attractive. This is only the beginning of a major push into Europe. Essentially the frontiers have been pushed back quite considerably.

The following is heard after the overlapping scenes finish:

I would show them to Joe in New York but it's only five in the morning. He's usually quite yielding when he's in bed but I don't think he'd want to start a whole new story.

Gilts

GRIMES *and his* MATE *in gilts dealing room of Klein Merrick.* SCILLA *on Liffe floor. Each has two phones.*

GRIMES (*to* MATE).
I'm long on these bastards.
MATE (*to* GRIMES).
3's a nice sell. They'd be above the mark.

GRIMES (*on phone*).
Scilla? Sell at 3.

SCILLA (*on two phones. To floor*).
10 at 3. 10 at 3.
(*On phone* 2.)
That's March is it?

MATE (*phone*).
6 Bid.

GRIMES (*phone*).
What you doing tonight?

SCILLA (*to floor*).
4 for 10. 4 for 10. Are you looking at me?
4 for 10.

GRIMES (*phone*).
Scilla?

SCILLA (*phone 1*).
Yes, we sold them.

GREVILLE (*phone*).
What you doing tonight?

SCILLA (*phone 1*).
Going out later – hang on.

(*Phone 2.*) 4 for 10 nothing doing. Will he go to 5?
(*To floor.*) 5 for 10! 5 for 10!

GRIMES (*phone 2*).
Bid 28 at the figure.

MATE (*to* GRIMES).
I'm only making a tick.

GRIMES (*to* MATE).
Leg out of it.

SCILLA (*phone*).
Grimes?

GRIMES (*to* MATE).
Futures are up.
(*Phone.*) Champagne bar / at six?

MATE (*phone*).
Selling one at the figure.
(*To* GRIMES.) I'm lifting a leg.

SCILLA (*phone 2*).
We got you 10 for 5 bid, OK?
(*Phone 1.*) Yes, champagne bar at 6.
(*Puts down phone 1, answers phone 2 again.*) Yes?

GRIMES (*phone 2*).
Get off the fucking line, will you please?

MATE (*to* GRIMES).
01 bid, 01 offered.

SCILLA (*phone 2*).
No, it's 5 bid at 6. I can't help you, I'm afraid.

GRIMES (*phone 1*).
Is it a seller or a buyer?
(*To* MATE.) He don't want to take us because he don't want to pay commission.

MATE (*phone 2*).
Offered at 4. Thanks very much but nothing done.

GRIMES (*phone 2 to* SCILLA).
5 March at 28.
(*To* MATE.) What are we long of?

SCILLA (*phone 1*).
No, it's gone to 29.

GRIMES (*to* MATE).
29 bid.
(*Phone 2.*) All right, 9 for 5.

SCILLA (*to floor*).
9 for 5! 9 for 5! / Terry!

MATE (*phone 1*).
You'd better keep up, I'll be off in a minute.

GRIMES (*phone 1*).
I'll make you a price, what do you want to do?

MATE (*to* GRIMES).
Bid 4.
(*Phone 1.*) I'm off, I'm off.

GRIMES (*to* MATE).
They was offered at 4.
(*Phone 1.*) Bid 3.

SCILLA (*phone 2*).
Three month sterling opened at 89.27 for March delivery and they've been trading in a 4 tick range.

MATE (*phone 2*).
Can't help you.
(*To* GRIMES.) There's a fucking seller trying to make us pay up.

GRIMES (*phone 2*).
Bid 3.

MATE (*to* GRIMES).
I think we should buy them.

GRIMES (*phone 1*).
Bid 4, bid 4 at 6.

SCILLA (*phone 2*).
No, it's quite quiet.
(*Phone 1.*) 9 for 5 a deal.

GRIMES.
You're getting good at this. Extra poo tonight.

MATE (*phone 1*).
2 bid at 5.
(*To* GRIMES.) Am I still cheap?

GRIMES (*to* MATE).
Sold 5 for 9 bid.

SCILLA (*phone 2*).
Looks as if they may finish at ·25.

MATE (*to* GRIMES).
What shall we do overnight?

GRIMES (*to* MATE).
I'll be long.

MATE (*to* GRIMES).
You don't want to be too long.

GRIMES (*phone* 2).
Closing out now at 4.

GRIMES *starts going down a list on a piece of paper marking prices.*

MATE (*to* GRIMES).
Doing the long end?

GRIMES (*to* MATE).
How shall I mark these, 2 or 3?

MATE (*to* GRIMES).
3.

GRIMES (*to* MATE).
Does it make a lot of difference to you?

MATE (*to* GRIMES).
Hundred thousand.

GRIMES (*to* MATE).
You must have made that trading in the last half hour.

SCILLA (*to floor*).
If you've lost any cards, Dave, I'm not helping you.

Paper.

JAKE *and another dealer sitting side by side. Two salespeople who shout from behind. Loud. American sound though they're not.*

SALES 1.
I tell you what else here. Sweden / just called.

SALES 2.
If you want to jump on the Hambro / bandwagon you better hurry.

JAKE (*phone*).
We also have two Japanese. I'll make those 88 6.

SALES 1.
Sweden first 10 has been called. How do we go these days?

DEALER (*phone*).
There's also an issue coming out again.

SALES 2.
The new BFC for World Bank.

DEALER (*to* JAKE).
I've just sold some paper / like that.

SALES 1 (*phone*).
They're not taking. I'll give you a level.

DEALER (*to* JAKE).
Shall we go ahead?

JAKE (*to* DEALER).
Let's wait a few / minutes before we have the whole world crashing down on us.

SALES 2.
Chase Corporation 68 88.
He can bash you in with one arm. He's got a black belt in karate.

SALES 1.
He's a very nice guy.

JAKE (*phone*).
What I suggested was swapping into something longer, threes or whatever.

DEALER (*phone*).
I've been talking to Hong Kong.

JAKE (*phone*).
Because / it's up to 14.

SALES 1.
We're waiting on the Bundesbank here.

JAKE (*phone*).
He doesn't care at the moment, / David.

SALES 2.
Paris intervention rate / still at 8%. Buy 10.

DEALER (*phone*).
It's done.

JAKE (*phone*).
Band two are at thirteen-sixteenths. It's a softer tone today.

DEALER (*to* JAKE).
He just said to me 590, I said it's done. He would have said 610 wouldn't he?

JAKE (*to* DEALER).
Get back on.

SALES 1.
We have Frankfurt here, Frankfurt, guys.
Discount rate remains 3%. Lombard 5. Buy twos / twos, twos, twos.

DEALER (*phone*).
He said to me 595 . . . OK that would be great.

SALES 2.
Tokyo one month 4.28125.

DEALER (*phone*).
Discretion is my middle name. Tell me tell me tell me tell me . . . you said you were going to tell me after lunch . . . / What, you bought some? It's

SALES 1.
He broke an arm wrestling with a treasury bond dealer.

DEALER.
going down . . . How fast do you want it to go down? . . . You're in profit, it's 7–8 right.

JAKE (*phone*).
Listen, guy. Listen listen listen listen listen.
Lombard Intervention steady at 5.

DEALER.
If it takes at 6 . . . no it's not going to take at 5 . . . if it goes to 7 . . . You're such a sleaze, you're not really a man of honour, you said you'd tell me after lunch . . . / I didn't know

SALES 2.
The guy dealt with Citibank but got back to them too late.

DEALER.
that's what your best was . . . tell me tell me . . . Futures are crashing off.

JAKE (*phone*).
The Mori poll put the Tories four up.

SALES 1.
We're going to lose power any minute, that's official.

DEALER.
What the fuck?

JAKE (*phone*).
So the three month interbank sterling rate – no it's a tick under –

SALES 1.
We have Milan three months 11½.

JAKE (*phone*).
There's a discrepancy between band 2 and band 3 . . . I thought it might give us some arbitrage possibilities.

DEALER (*phone*).
Come on come on come on guy.

SALES 1.
What's with the ECU linked deposits for Nomura?

SALES 2.
Now hurry hurry hurry guys hurry.

Power goes – no screens, no phones.

Outcry.

JAKE.
Marvellous.

DEALER.
If the market moves in a big way we'll get cremated.

JAKE.
They left us a whole lot of orders we're meant to be filling.

DEALER.
I have to speak to Zurich.

SALES 2.
So what happens now?

SALES 1.
They go elsewhere, bozo.

Liffe Champagne Bar

SCILLA (*trader with Liffe*), *her brother* JAKE (*commercial paper dealer*), GRIMES (*gilts dealer*) *drinking together in the champagne bar.*

GRIMES.
Offered me sixty right? So next day
The other lot seventy-five. OK,
So I go to the boss and go 'I don't want to trouble
You', and he goes 'All right you cunt,
Don't mess about, how much do you want?'
So I go – I mean why not – I go 'Double
What I'm getting now', and he goes 'fuck off'. Meanwhile
Zackerman rings and – this'll make you smile –
He goes, he goes, I'll give you a hundred grand,
Plus the car and that, and fifty in your hand,
But no thinking about it, no calling back,
This is my first and last. I say, Zac,
A good dealer don't need time to think.
So there you go. Have another drink.

JAKE.
So there's twenty-seven firms dealing gilts.

SCILLA.
Where there used to be two.

GRIMES.
Half the bastards don't know what to do.

JAKE.
Those of you that do have got it made.
SCILLA.
And all twenty-seven want ten per cent of the trade.
GRIMES.
So naturally there's going to be blood spilt.
JAKE.
Ten per cent? Go in there and get fifty.
SCILLA.
Everyone thinks it's Christmas and it's great to know they love you,
But you mustn't forget there's plenty still above you.
(There's at least two dozen people in the City now getting a million a year.)
Think of the ones at the top who can afford
To pay us to make them money, and they're on the board.
GRIMES.
They're for the chop.
JAKE (*simultaneously*).
I'm on the board.
SCILLA.
True, you're on the board,
But how many of us will make it to the top?
If we've a Porsche in the garage and champagne in the glass
We don't notice there's a lot of power still held by men of daddy's class.
GRIMES.
No but most of them got no feel
For the market. Jake's the only public schoolboy what can really deal.
JAKE.
That's because I didn't go to university and learn to think twice.
SCILLA.
Yes, but they regard us as the SAS.
They send us in to smash the place up and get them out of a mess.
GRIMES.
Listen, do you want my advice?
SCILLA.
They'll have us on the scrap heap at thirty-five,
JAKE.
I've no intention of working after I'm thirty.

SCILLA.
Unless we're really determined to survive
(which I am).

JAKE.
It probably means you have to fight dirty.

GRIMES.
Listen, Nomura's recruiting a whole lot of Sloanes.
Customers like to hear them on the phones
Because it don't sound Japanese.
If you want to get in somewhere big –

SCILLA.
Grimes, don't be such a sleaze.
Daddy could have got me in at the back door
But you know I'd rather be working on the floor.
I love it down with the oiks, it's more exciting.

JAKE.
When Scilla was little she always enjoyed fighting
(better at it than me).

SCILLA.
But it's time to go it alone and be a local.
I'm tired of making money for other people.

GRIMES.
(Going to make a million a year?

SCILLA.
I might do.)

GRIMES.
I tell you what though, Zackerman can recruit
The very best because he's got the loot.

JAKE. I told him for what he's getting from my team, why be a meanie?
He got rid of the BMW's and got us each a Lamborghini.
He's quite a useful guy to have as a friend.
So I thought I'd ask him home for the weekend.
He's talking to dad about amalgamation.
Klein needs a brokers'.

SCILLA.
And Daddy needs a banker.

GRIMES.
Won't survive without one, poor old wanker.

JAKE.
I told Dad / his best bet's a conglomeration.

GRIMES.
Some of them old brokers is real cunts.

JAKE.
But I've got to go to Frankfurt Friday night,
So Scilla, you can drive him down, all right?

SCILLA.
Yes, that's fine. I wonder if he hunts.

JAKE *leaves.*

SCILLA.
I'm beginning to find Zackerman quite impressive.
(I wonder how he got to where he is now?)

GRIMES.
My school reports used to say I was too aggressive
(but it's come in quite useful).
My old headmaster wouldn't call me a fool again.
I got a transfer fee like a footballer. He thought I was a hooligan.
He goes, you fool boy, you're never going to get to work,
What use is a CSE in metalwork?
I could kiss his boots the day he kicked me out of school.

GRIMES *and* SCILLA *leave.*
ZAC *enters.*

ZAC.
So cut the nostalgia. I'm the guy they're talking about, Zac.
I'm here for my bank, Klein Merrick, to buy up jobbers and brokers.
And turn the best of them into new market makers.
The first time I realised how fast things were changing was something that happened at Klein's in New York a few years back.

MERRISON, *a banker, co-chief executive officer of Klein Merrick.*
DURKFELD, *a trader, co-chief executive officer of Klein Merrick.*

MERRISON.
So I told them 83 was a great year,
Profits up ten million on 82.
But we can do better than that by far.
Leveraged buyouts are the way to go
(I told them).
Take Krafft, put up three million to acquire Hoffman Clocks,
Borrowed the rest of the fifty million, a year later makes a public offering, and pockets a whole fifty million plus he retains thirty

million of stock.
That's eighty million dollars on his initial three.
And that's from taking a risk instead of a fee.
We advise other people on acquisitions.
They make the serious money. Fuck it all.
The company should take its own positions.
Partners should be willing to risk their own capital.
I told them, man is a gambling animal.
Risk is one of our company traditions.
Old Benny Klein took risks, the latest news
Meant profit, they'd say on Wall Street 'Let the Jews
Have that one,' and he would. Imagine the scene,
Guy comes and says 'I can make flying machines.'
Benny puts up the money, doesn't bat an eye,
He says, 'OK, so make the machines fly.'
When I was working with Henry under Nixon

DURKFELD.
Jack, I heard this speech before.

MERRISON.
There were quite a few things needed fixing –

DURKFELD.
Jack, I heard it already.

MERRISON.
So, I'm a bore.
Tell me, do you have a problem, Eddie?
I trust you've no more trouble with your wife?
It's a while since you took a good vacation.
None of us gets enough relaxation
(I never even make it upstairs to the gym get a massage).
Tell me what you want out of life.

DURKFELD.
I'm a simple guy, Jack. I walk in the woods
And shoot things. I don't talk so good
As you, I'm good on my own, I shoot straight,
I don't say, 'Shall I, shan't I?' You guys deliberate
One hell of a lot. I walk on my own
And I know I could run this show on my own.

MERRISON.
I'm not sure I understand what you're saying.

DURKFELD.
I don't have the same alternatives
A guy like you does. You say Henry

Where I say Kissinger. You want to move?
You've talked about some possibility.
For me, this is enough.
I don't look beyond this company.
You ready to go do that stuff?

MERRISON.
Let me understand what you're saying here.

DURKFELD.
I want to go solo running Klein.
I'm saying I'm suggesting you resign.

MERRISON.
I just promoted you.

DURKFELD.
Should I be grateful?

MERRISON.
I made you my equal.

DURKFELD.
Jack. I hate you.
Didn't you know that? You're not so smart.
You're too important to smell your own fart.

MERRISON.
Eddie. I need to understand your problem.

DURKFELD.
There's guys don't want me in their club.
I don't give a rat's ass.
Those guys would have looked the other way
And let the cattle trucks pass.
(I don't want to play golf with those bastards. I don't even play golf. I can walk without hitting a ball.)
I'm good at my job.
I stay on the floor with the guys.
Screw the panelling, screw the Picassos, I am not interested in office size.
(You like lunch, you have lunch.)
I run the best trading floor in New York City,
And traders make two dollars profit for this company for every dollar made by you bankers.
And you treat us like a load of shit.
You make me your equal, I'm meant to say thanks
For that? Thanks, Jack. Come off it.
I make this company eighty million dollars and bankers pocket most of that profit.
Bankers get on the cover of *Time*.

MERRISON.
Brother, can you spare a dime?
DURKFELD.
I do OK, sure, I'm not talking greed.
I'm talking how I mean to succeed.
(My father came to this country – forget it.)
Which of us does this company need?
I'm talking indispensable.
MERRISON.
And my father? You think I'm some kind of patrician?
I was sweeping floors in my uncle's delicatessen
So don't –
The company needs us both. Be sensible.
There's two aspects to the institution.
Nobody means to imply they underestimate your invaluable contribution.
I need to understand what you're saying here so let's set a time we can have a further talk.
DURKFELD.
You don't seem to get it. You're sitting in my chair. Walk.
ZAC. And the guy walked.
(He walked with twenty million dollars but he walked.)
The financial world won't be the same again
Because the traders are coming down the fast lane.
They don't even know it themselves, they're into fucking or getting a Porsche, getting a Porsche *and* a Mercedes Benz.
But you can't drive two cars at once.
If you're making the firm ten million you want a piece of the action.
You know you've got it made the day you're offered stock options.
There are guys that blow out, sure, stick too much whitener up their nose.
Guy over forty's got any sense he takes his golden handshake and goes.
Because the new guys are hungrier and hornier,
They're Jews from the Bronx and spicks from Southern California.
It's like Darwin says, survival of the fit,
Now, here in England, it's just beginning to hit.
The British Empire was a cartel.
England could buy whatever it wanted cheap

And make a profit on what it made to sell.
The empire's gone but the City of London keeps
On running like a cartoon cat off a cliff – bang.
That's your Big Bang.
End of the City cartel.
Swell.
England's been fucking the world with interest but now it's a different scene.
I don't mind bending over and greasing my ass but I sure ain't using my own vaseline.
Now as a place to live, England's swell.
Tokyo treats me like a slave, New York trics to kill me, Hong Kong
I have to turn a blind eye to the suffering and I feel wrong.
London, I go to the theatre, I don't get mugged, I have classy friends,
And I go see them in the country at the weekends.

The meet of a hunt. On horses are ZAC, GREVILLE, *stockbroker, his daughter* SCILLA, *and other hunt members, e.g.,* MRS CARRUTHERS, LADY VERE, MAJOR *and* FARMER. FROSBY, *jobber, comes in late, on foot to watch.*

MRS CARRUTHERS.
The hound that I walked goes up front with the best.

FARMER.
The best of the pack is that cunning old bitch.

LADY VERE.
His fetlocks swell up so I'll give him a rest.

MAJOR.
Went over his neck and headfirst in the ditch.

GREVILLE.
Stand still will you dammit, whatever's the matter?

MAJOR.
Bottle of sherry he won in a raffle.

LADY VERE.
Hunt saboteurs made a terrible clatter.

MRS CARRUTHERS.
You can't hold her, Greville, in only a snaffle.

FARMER.
It's colder today but the going's much quicker

SCILLA.
Jumped onto the lawn and straight over the vicar.

GREVILLE.
Good morning
MAJOR.
Good morning
GREVILLE.
Good morning
MRS CARRUTHERS.
Hello
GREVILLE.
Good morning
LADY VERE.
Good morning
GREVILLE.
I don't think you know
Mr Zackerman here, my colleague and guest.
MRS CARRUTHERS.
The hound that I walked goes up front with the best.
GREVILLE.
Mr Zackerman wanted to join us of course
And Mrs Carruthers provided a horse.
MRS CARRUTHERS.
He's terribly clever, won't put a foot wrong,
When he hears the horn blow he'll be off like a rocket.
His mouth's rather hard and he is very strong,
Don't fight him, he'll pull out your arms by the socket.
There's not a horse safer and not a horse faster,
So don't step on hounds and don't override master.
LADY VERE.
Making the most of the beautiful weather.
GREVILLE.
American fellow, a friend of my daughter,
Colleague of mine, we'll be working together.
SCILLA.
Left behind at the gate and came off in the water.
FARMER.
The best of the pack is that cunning old bitch.
MAJOR.
Went over his neck and headfirst in the ditch.
LADY VERE.
Hunt saboteurs made a terrible clatter.

GREVILLE.
Stand still will you dammit, whatever's the matter?
Priscilla insists upon working for Liffe.
I was terribly doubtful and so was my wife.
(The London International Financial Futures Exchange, terrible place, full of the most frightful yobs.)
Hardly the spot for a daughter of mine
But she buys her own horses and takes her own line.

LADY VERE.
We've lost our head gardener, bit of a chore.

MAJOR.
I'm sure Mr Zimmerman's hunted before.

ZAC.
Not a great deal but I have been out a few times in Ireland with the Galway Blazers.

LADY VERE.
In that case I'm sure you can give us a lead.

MRS CARRUTHERS.
The girl's putting far too much oat in his feed.

SCILLA.
Is it true?

ZAC.
Well I saw both the start and the finish.
I was on foot drinking plenty of Guinness.

SCILLA.
There aren't any gates and I'm not waiting for you.

ZAC.
You're so tenderhearted, that's why I adore you.

FARMER.
It's colder today but the going's much quicker

SCILLA.
Jumped onto the lawn and straight over the vicar.
(So Klein have taken over Daddy. How long will he last? Five years?)

ZAC.
(He could be lucky.)

GREVILLE.
Not joining us Frosby? Find horses a bore?

MRS CARRUTHERS.
He's terribly clever, won't put a foot wrong.

LADY VERE.
We've lost our head gardener, bit of a chore.
CARRUTHERS.
His mouth's rather hard and he is very strong.
FROSBY.
I like a stroll to see the meet.
I'm happier on my own two feet.
Is that chap there the American?
GREVILLE.
Yes, it's Klein's Zac Zackerman.
FROSBY (*to himself*).
Yanks go home. Yanks are robbers.
GREVILLE.
Zac, I want you to meet a colleague I've done a great deal of business with over the years, one of the jobbers.
Mr Frosby, Mr Zackerman.
ZAC.
Hi Mr Frosby, I can't really talk.
This horse won't stand still and he won't even walk.
MRS CARRUTHERS.
When he hears the horn blow he'll be off like a rocket.
Don't fight him, he'll pull out your arms by the socket.
GREVILLE.
No more long lunches for me, Frosby, no more lying in bed.
It's up at six now in the godforsaken
Dark cold mornings. On the bright side
The company does an excellent egg and bacon.
FROSBY.
Some things change, some things don't end.
After all, a friend's a friend.
MRS CARRUTHERS.
So don't step on hounds and don't override master.
ZAC.
Is this horse going to do what I tell it Priscilla?
MRS CARRUTHERS.
There's not a horse safer and not a horse faster.
SCILLA.
It's generally known around here as a killer.
ZAC.
(When I end up in bed with a broken leg I only hope you're going to look after me.)

SCILLA.
(Drop dead, bozo.)
The horn blows.
They all go in a rush, leaving FROSBY *alone.*

FROSBY.
The stock exchange was a village street.
You strolled about and met your friends.
Now we never seem to meet.
I don't get asked much at weekends.

Everyone had a special name.
We really had a sense of humour.
And everybody played the game.
You learned a thing or two from rumour.

Since Big Bang the floor is bare,
They deal in offices on screens.
But if the chap's not really there
You can't be certain what he means.

I've been asked to retire early.
The firm's not doing awfully well.
I quite enjoy the hurly burly.
Sitting alone at home is hell.

I can't forgive Greville. He's gone with that Yankee bank buying its way in, that Yak, Whack, whatsisname, Zac, trying to keep up with his children. His son Jake's one of these so-called marketmakers. Some of us have been making markets for thirty years. And his daughter Scilla works with those barrow boys in Liffe you'd expect to see on a street corner selling Christmas paper and cheap watches, they earn more than I do, they won't last.

I have a constant funny ache.
I can't see straight because of grief.
I really think my heart will break.
Revenge would give me some relief.

So now I'll phone the DTI,
Who want a clean and honest City.
Jake's no better than a thief
And why should I have any pity?
I've cried and now my friends can cry.

I've had the odd tip from Greville, I know he gets it from Jake and there's far more than I ever see. Let the DTI investigate. The City's not mine any more so let it fall.

I love the masters in their pink
I'm glad traditions still exist.

I think I'll go and have a drink.
I love the valley in the mist.
(I'm very frightened.)

ZAC *phones* TK *and* MARYLOU BAINES *in New York*.

TK.
This is Marylou Baines' personal assistant.

ZAC.
It's Zac, I've got to speak to her this instant.
I know it's 3 a.m. your time, but I know she's awake.
Tell her it's about Jake.

TK.
Hi, Zac, this is TK here. Can I help you? What's the problem? Is it urgent?

ZAC.
Stop talking like a tubful of detergent /.
I got to speak to her now and not now but five minutes ago.

MARYLOU.
Zac, is there something I should know?

ZAC.
Jake's dead. They think it's suicide.

MARYLOU.
Thank you, Zac.
Jake was a nice guy but I haven't heard from him since some time back.

She hangs up and speaks to TK.

MARYLOU.
Put anything from Jake Todd in the shredder.

ZAC *phones* JACINTA CONDOR *in London*.

ZAC.
Jacinta, it's me. / Bad news. Jake's been found shot. /
It looks like suicide because he was in some kind of trouble with the DTI / though so far nobody seems to know exactly what.

JACINTA. Zac! What? My God.
He was the English colleague I like the most (except for you).
I hope I never meet his unhappy ghost.
I look forward to meeting. /

JACINTA *phones* NIGEL AJIBALA.

JACINTA.
Nigel, have you read the newspapers today?

NIGEL.
No, what's the matter?

JACINTA.
Don't panic, OK?

This overlaps with CORMAN *phoning* ZAC.

CORMAN.
Zac, have you seen the fucking *Times* this morning?
Why didn't Todd give us any warning?
Why didn't he tell us about the DTI?
Do you think he's talked?

ZAC.
Deny. Deny. Deny.
(Let them see what they can prove.)

This overlaps with JACINTA *phoning* MARYLOU.

JACINTA.
Marylou, the delivery. You think we should wait a week?

MARYLOU.
Hold off for twenty-four hours, OK? We'll speak.

NIGEL *phones* CORMAN.

NIGEL.
Mr Corman, I'm deeply shocked that anyone associated with your company should be touched by the slightest breath / of scandal.

CORMAN.
The deal's in no way affected by his death.
(The deal is the priority.)

This overlaps with MARYLOU *phoning* ZAC.

MARYLOU.
Zac, your news is causing a certain amount of tension.

ZAC.
Can we still rely / on you?

MARYLOU.
Sure, but never mention.

CORMAN *phones* MARYLOU *and gets* TK *on answering machine*.

CORMAN.
TK? Marylou?

TK (*on machine*).
Hello, this is the office of Marylou Baines. I'm afraid Ms Baines is not available right now to come to the phone,
But if you wish to leave a message for her or for TK, her

personal assistant, please speak for as long as you wish after the tone.

CORMAN.
Fuck.

ZAC.
I went with Scilla to identify her brother Jake's body which was kind of a mess.
Then we stopped for coffee, which was making me late for work, but it was a special occasion, I guess.
It'd be good if we could handle this
So you don't get associated with anything too scandalous.
(Just stick to No comment, and let them make things up.)

SCILLA.
Zac, I told the police I had breakfast with Jake at Klein Merrick yesterday morning.
Just to say hello. But in fact he gave me a warning.

ZAC.
They know the DTI paid him a visit.

SCILLA.
But it wasn't just that. He was frightened of . . .

ZAC.
Well, what is it?

SCILLA.
What was Jake like? charming, clever, idle.
He won, he lost, he cheated a bit, he treated it all as a game.
Can you really imagine him killing himself for shame?
(He didn't know what honour meant.)
He wasn't telling me he was suicidal,
He was telling me . . . You may think it's absurd, but
I'm certain he must have been murdered.

JAKE *and* SCILLA *at breakfast.*

JAKE.
Don't let me worry you, I'm probably imagining it.

SCILLA.
Have you shared a needle?

JAKE.
Not Aids, I'm perfectly / healthy.

SCILLA.
At work they ask for tea in an Aids cup, they mean / a disposable because the dishwasher –

JAKE.
Listen, I've a problem. Listen.

SCILLA.
What?

JAKE.
No, never mind, you know I left my diary at your place last week? / You haven't got it on you?

SCILLA.
Yes, do you want – ?
No, but I could – .

JAKE.
Hold onto it. No, maybe you'd better – No, hold onto it. You can always burn it later. Fine.

SCILLA.
What is this?

JAKE.
No, it's just . . . I'm in a spot of bother with the authorities / but it's no problem. I'm sorting it

SCILLA.
What have you done?

JAKE.
out, it's more what the sorting out might lead to / because once I start –

SCILLA.
Are you going to prison?

JAKE.
No, I'm not going to be in trouble at all by the look of it but that's the problem, I'm going to be very – I'm probably paranoid about this.

SCILLA.
Leave the country. / Are you serious?

JAKE.
They've taken my passport. I just wanted to let you know in case anything –. I haven't mentioned any of this to Dad / but when the shit hits –

SCILLA.
No, don't get Dad started. Can I do anything?

JAKE.
No, it's all under control. I feel better talking to you. I didn't go to bed, you know how you get in the night. / If anything happens to me –

SCILLA.
Have some more coffee.
What? Like what?

JAKE.
Shall I get you another croissant?

SCILLA.
So what have they found out?

JAKE.
Jam with it?

SCILLA.
If you've been making a fortune, I think it's very unfair of you not to have let me in on it.

JAKE.
Forget it.

SCILLA.
So you haven't got Aids. That's great.

SCILLA *and* ZAC *continue.*

SCILLA.
So clearly he was frightened because he'd agreed to tell the DTI
who else was involved
(and they'd want to shut him up).
If I can find out who they are, the murder's halfway solved.
There's plenty of names and numbers here in his diary
So I'll start by contacting anyone who looks interesting and making my own inquiry.

ZAC.
Are you OK?

SCILLA.
Yes, I feel terrific.

ZAC.
You'll just find out a whole lot of colleagues' numbers, that won't tell you anything specific.
My number's probably there for God's sake.

SCILLA.
I'm going to find out who killed Jake.

ZAC.
Take a sedative, have a sleep, and then see how you feel.

SCILLA.
Nobody sleeps in the middle of a deal.

ZAC.
You've always been lucky, Scilla, don't abuse it.
(I mean, these guys, whoever they are, they could be dangerous.)
You're crazy at the moment, / you're in shock.

SCILLA.
/ I'm in shock, I might as well use it.
(I'll let you know what happens.)

ZAC.
Jake's death was a shock for me too, and I kept thinking about a friend of his I'd just met.
She was called Jacinta Condor and we'd all been doing business together and I knew she'd be quite upset.

ZAC *phones.*

ZAC.
I want to order a number of tropical birds . . .
Maybe twenty? . . .
Don't tell me what kinds because I won't have heard . . .
Yeah, parrots, cockatoos, marmosets (no, is that a monkey?) lovebirds, sure, stick in some lovebirds, an assortment in good bright colours, I don't care the exact number but plenty . . .
No not a cage so much as a small aviary . . .
Deliver it gift wrapped to Jacinta Condor, at the Savoy and the card should read, 'From Zac, as a small tribute to your beauty and bravery.'

SCILLA *and* GREVILLE *at* GREVILLE'*s house.*

SCILLA.
Pull yourself together, Daddy.
What does it matter if Jake was a baddy?

GREVILLE.
Poor boy. Who would have thought? I'd rather he'd been a failure.
He used to want to emigrate and sheepfarm in Australia.
He always would rush in. He had no sense of balance.
He could have done anything, you know, he had so many talents.
Musician. Politician. No obstacles in his way.
If he'd done something else, he'd be alive today.

SCILLA.
What was he up to, Daddy?
If it was just insider dealing,
It's not a proper crime like stealing.
They say it's a crime without a victim.
He'd hardly kill himself just because the DTI nicked him.

GREVILLE.

Dammit, why should he die for something that's not a crime?
(It's not illegal in America, Switzerland, Japan, it's only been illegal here the last few years.)
You have to use what you know. You do it all the time.
That used to be the way you made a reputation.
By having first class contacts, and first class information.
One or two greedy people attracted attention to it.
Suddenly we all pretend Englishmen don't do it.

SCILLA.

So what was he up to, Daddy?

GREVILLE.

I've simply no idea.

SCILLA.

Do you know who these people are? I've got Jake's diary here.
Marylou Baines.

GREVILLE.

Marylou Baines
Was originally a poor girl from the plains.
She set out to make whatever she wanted hers
And now she's one of America's top arbitrageurs
(second only to Boesky).

SCILLA.

Condor, Jacinta.

GREVILLE.

A very smart lady from South America who comes here every winter.
Europe sends aid, her family says thanks
And buys Eurobonds in Swiss banks.

SCILLA.

Corman.

GREVILLE.

Billy Corman,
William the Conqueror, the great invader,
A very highly successful dawn raider.
I don't want to hear any more. Did Jake have friends like this?
I wish he was still a baby and giving daddy a kiss.

SCILLA.

Pull yourself together, daddy.
Did he give you information?

GREVILLE.

Absolutely not.

SCILLA.
I thought you might be in on it.

GREVILLE.
In on what?

SCILLA.
Then aren't you annoyed he kept it secret from you and didn't share what he'd got?

GREVILLE.
Scilla –

SCILLA.
Jake had powerful friends, that's clear from what you said.
And that means powerful enemies who'd like to see him dead. /
(He wasn't brave enough to kill himself.)

GREVILLE.
Absolute nonsense.

SCILLA.
I'll start by calling on Corman.

GREVILLE.
Security's terribly tight /
He'll never agree to see you.

SCILLA.
Don't worry. I'll get in somehow and see if it gives him a fright.

GREVILLE.
Scilla, you don't seem to realise. Newspapers across the nation.
I could easily lose my job if I lose my reputation.
You and the yobs you work with are hardly worth a mention
(no one expects them to have any standards),
But I have to keep very quiet, and not attract attention.
Until it's all blown over I think I'll stay in bed.

SCILLA.
You never liked me, Daddy. Jake was always your favourite.

GREVILLE.
I don't like the louts you work with.

SCILLA.
And now you've got to pay for it.

GREVILLE.
Poor Scilla, are you suffering from feelings of rejection?

SCILLA.
If I find out you were in on it, you're not getting my protection.

GREVILLE.
(In on killing Jakey?)

SCILLA.
(In on anything.)

GREVILLE.
Darling, don't be difficult when I'm so awfully sad.
I think Jakey was playing in a bigger league than Dad.

SCILLA.
I've always been ashamed of you. Your drink and your pomposity.

GREVILLE.
Scilla, the oiks you work with have made you a monstrosity.

SCILLA.
If I find you're implicated in my investigation / the *News of the World* can have you.

GREVILLE.
Darling, you always did have a vivid imagination
(like poor Mummy).

ZAC.
When I left Scilla I rushed back to work because Corman's bid for Albion was just reaching its peak.
He'd been spending the night in the office the whole of that week.
We'd been building to this since the day a few months ago
When Albion started, just one of several deals, easy and slow.
It started like this:

CORMAN *a corporate raider*. BROWN *and* SMITH, *industrial spies*. ZAC. MRS ETHERINGTON, *a stockbroker*.

CORMAN.
The analysts' reports are satisfactory,
Predicting high industrial synergy.
I'll have to close the chocolate biscuit factory.
The management lacks drive and energy.
Tell me what you learnt about the company.

BROWN.
I spent a week posing as a secretary.
The working atmosphere is very pleasant.
A shock to the chairman would be salutary,
His presence at his desk is just symbolic,
He disappears to fish and shoot pheasant.
The managing director's alcoholic,
But still he's everybody's favourite,
His drink 'n' driving ends him up in court,
He gets the company to pay for it.
The middle management are sound but lazy,

The details will be found in my report.
The chief of marketing is going crazy.

CORMAN.
Excellent, they'll put up no resistance.
I'll sack them all, put in new staff, maybe promote a few of their assistants.
Too late for them to make the company over,
Because I am going to take the company over.
Now to the larger and still more inviting
Albion Products. Fuck the analysts,
What do they know? It's that much more exciting.
Is their chairman gaga too and their managing director always pissed?

SMITH.
No, he's sober and quite competent.
Duckett runs a rather happy ship.
I hear the head of sales is impotent,
A very old director broke his hip,
Apart from that they all seem quite efficient.
Employees feel considerable loyalty.
The factory has been visited by royalty.

CORMAN.
Albion is obviously deficient
In management. Old-fashioned and paternal.
These figures stink. I can make it earn a l-
ot more for its shareholders, who are
The owners after all. It will be far
Better run, streamlined, rationalised,
When it forms part of Corman Enterprise.
(And anyway I want it.)
Right. Both targets will be hit.
Now summon my war cabinet.

CORMAN.
Zac, I really like this company.

ZAC.
It'll take some stalking. It's a big confident beast.

CORMAN.
But I'm told you're a takeover artiste.
Can you get it for me?

ZAC.
Corman, you're the buyer. /
I pride myself I can acquire any company the client

CORMAN.
Anyway, if it was easy it'd bore me.
ZAC.
may desire.
(If I was defending Albion you wouldn't stand a chance.)
We're going to need a whole lot of finance from somewhere.
CORMAN.
Zackerman, that's your ride on the funfair.
Now Etherington. I want you to start a stealthy
Purchase of Albion stock. Don't frighten them.
The price must hardly move, just look quite healthy.
We'll put nooses round their necks and suddenly tighten them.
ETHERINGTON.
Albion's price is three hundred and ten.
I shall acquire twenty million ordinary
Shares on your behalf, imperceptibly.
And I shall let you know of any change.
ZAC.
We've got to get out here and ride the range.
ETHERINGTON.
I don't think you'll find me lacking in assiduity.
CORMAN.
I'm a great admirer of Etherington's ingenuity.
(Top brokers for fuck's sake, what do you think I am? Brokers to royalty.)
When we tell Duckett I own five per cent
(plus what else I'll control by then)
He'll suddenly wonder where his company went.

DUCKETT.
DUCKETT.
I'm Duckett. I enjoy the *Financial Times*.
It's fun reading about other people's crimes.
My company Albion's price is looking perky.
I think I'll buy that villa in the south of Turkey.

CORMAN, ETHERINGTON, ZAC.
CORMAN.
So what's on the agenda today?
Let's get all the rubbish out of the way.
ETHERINGTON.
We're failing to acquire Mayfield.

CORMAN.
Except I never fail.
Why don't I suggest we'll leave them alone, provided they pay us greenmail?
(American term, greenbacks, blackmail, everybody happy?)

ZAC.
If they really want to defend themselves they'll do a leveraged management buyout to get back their shares.

ETHERINGTON.
So we make a hundred million.

CORMAN.
And the lousy company's still theirs.

ZAC.
(Plus a whole lot of debt.
In the US there's an oil company borrowed four billion dollars to fight off T. Boone Pickens and now they're paying three million a day interest.)

CORMAN.
So that money goes to improving our position
With Albion, my favourite acquisition.
How we doing?

ETHERINGTON.
The Albion share is up to three fifteen
And you now own 4.9% /
Not 5%, so no need to disclose.

CORMAN.
Excellent.
So now?

ETHERINGTON.
Now we contact institutions,
The pension fund managers who hold
Millions of Corman shares and indicate
It would be wise to lend us their support.

ZAC.
Can we rely on them?

ETHERINGTON.
They won't say no,
For otherwise a succulent new issue
Next time we have one might not come their way.

CORMAN.
It's their duty to keep our price up after all.
The poor old pensioners won't want it to fall.
ETHERINGTON.
We also intimate it's in their interest
To buy up Albion so that more and more
Albion shares belong to friends of ours. /
A fan club and not a concert party.
ZAC.
A concert party.
CORMAN.
Come on, don't fart
About, it's a concert party.
ETHERINGTON.
A fan club (of disinterested supporters) is respectable and legal.
A concert party (of people you've induced to support you) reprehensible.
This is a line you may trust us to tread /
(as long as necessary)
CORMAN.
Tread in the shit. Tread where you need to tread.
Now purchases must also be made by Metgee, Upkate,
Battershot, Mountainring
ZAC.
and Stoneark.
CORMAN.
Five nominee companies registered in the Turks and Caicos Islands, Panama and Sark.
They can each acquire 4.9%.
ZACKERMAN.
And one of our problems is solved.
You'll acquire a huge share in Albion without anyone suspecting you're involved.
ETHERINGTON.
We're still left with a cashflow problem.
Albion's more than three times as big as Corman.
CORMAN.
Zac, you understand how a buyer works.
Time you stepped in and showed us a few fireworks.
ZAC.
The last couple of years in the United States it's been takeover mania

And I guess the deals there have gotten somewhat zanier.
Junk bonds are a quick way of raising cash, but it's kind of a hit 'n' run method, which doesn't go down too well in Britain.
You don't have millions of private investors crazy to gamble on debt.

ETHERINGTON.
No, you wouldn't succeed with junk bonds here just yet.
But the British public's financial education
Is going in leaps and bounds with privatisation.
Sid will buy junk soon. / Just wait.

ZAC.
Great.

CORMAN.
So no junk. How do we stand with the loan?
Can you show us some tricks?

ZAC.
The money can be supplied from a number of banks here and in the United States led by our own.
I got the rate of interest down a couple of ticks.
In return they want us to mortgage Upkate, Battershot and Stoneark, and form five new nominee companies so we can wind up Albion and redistribute its assets,
Which gives us tax neutral benefits.
We repay the loan and the interest by selling off certain sections of Albion after it's been acquired.

CORMAN.
Some people might think I'm a touch overgeared.
Our ratio of debt to equity is – ?

ETHERINGTON.
Four hundred per cent.

CORMAN.
Taking into account the billion and a half you've lent.
(But being in debt is the best way to be rich.)

ZAC.
(America's national debt is over a trillion dollars.)

CORMAN.
So we've got the money. (*To* ETHERINGTON.) Get out there and spend it.
We've got Albion.

ZAC.
No, let's wait and see how Duckett's going to defend it.
(Poison pills? shark repellent?)

ETHERINGTON.
If Albion's shares should fall some of our friends would be in for a shock.

ZAC.
A deposit with us could provide a guarantee.

CORMAN.
And then there's the question of buying Corman stock.
To buy your own shares is illegal and cannot be.

ZAC.
But the bank can buy them, no problem and we'll let you know later about our fee.

CORMAN.
Zackerman, my very sincere thanks.
This is the kind of service I expect from our banks.
Etherington, I'm sure you've plenty to do.
I'll join you later for a glass of poo.

ETHERINGTON *goes.*

We don't breathe a word of this to anyone.
But someone could breathe a word to Marylou.
I think she could step in here and have some fun.
But I don't want direct contact and nor should you.

ZAC.
No problem.

CORMAN *goes.*

So I called Jake Todd.

ZAC *and* JAKE *drinking in champagne bar. Late night. Both drunk.*

JAKE.
What did you think of the family?

ZAC.
Quite a mansion.

JAKE.
You could buy yourself something equally handsome.
(Or three.)

ZAC.
Why do the British always want land?
(In Paris or New York you live in an apartment, why do the English need gardens?)

JAKE.
You're not upper class without it, you're too American to understand.

ZAC.
You don't make money out of land, you make money out of money.

JAKE.
It's a dream. Woods. Springtime. Owning the spring.
What's so funny?

ZAC.
Is that your dream?

JAKE.
I never dream. / (I never sleep)

ZAC.
Because it's come to an end.
Young kids like you making money now – and I mean the ones who've never had it, not like you – they're going to come up with new ways to spend
Because they're going to come up with new dreams.

JAKE.
I'll tell you, Zac, sometimes it seems . . .

ZAC.
What?

JAKE.
I don't know, what were we saying?

ZAC.
When?

JAKE.
Forget it.

ZAC.
Tell you something, Jake. Give Albion some attention.

JAKE.
I could get on the blower to Marylou / and just give it a mention.

ZAC.
Don't tell me.

JAKE.
Tell you something. I fancy the ocean.
Instead of land. I'd like to own a big cube of sea, right down to the bottom, all the fish, weeds, the lot.
There'd be takers for that.

ZAC.
Sure, it's a great notion.

JAKE.
  Or air. Space. A square metre going straight up into infinity.
ZAC.
  And a section of God at the top.
JAKE.
  Oh yes, I'll make you a market in divinity (any day).

MARYLOU BAINES *and* TK *in New York*.
TK.
  There's a message from Jake Todd in London.
  He recommends buying shares in Albion.
MARYLOU.
  Can I take it this is so far completely secret?
TK.
  Yes, when it gets out it'll really move the market.
MARYLOU.
  Are you trading in this stock on your own account?
TK.
  Not for a very considerable amount.
MARYLOU.
  You'll soon be setting up your own show.
TK.
  No, Ms Baines, I wouldn't go, you taught me everything I know.
  I really admire your style, Miss Baines.
  (You're a great American.)
MARYLOU.
  Sure, arbitrage is a service to the community,
  And it's too bad they're prosecuting people you'd have thought would have had immunity.
  By buying and selling large amounts of stock we ensure the market's liquidity –
  I work twenty-four hours a day and take pills for stomach acidity –
  So companies can be taken over easy,
  Which means discharging superfluous workers, discontinuing unprofitable lines, the kind of stuff that makes your lazy inefficient management queasy.
  So considering the good we do the US economy,
  I reckon we should be treated with a little more respect and bonhomie.
  I have a hundred and fifty telephone lines because I depend on information.

TK.

(What's the least a person could start with?

MARYLOU.

I started small – say twenty?)

You need to know what's going on in businesses all over the nation,

TK.

(And Britain)

MARYLOU.

You take a lot of gambles, / which keeps the adrenalin flowing and is why it's known as risk arbitrage,

TK.

(Ms Baines, I admire your guts)

MARYLOU.

Though if you know how to get the right information the risk isn't all that large.

TK.

But since Boesky was caught out –

MARYLOU.

Sure, some of our informants are more cautious,

But information's what it's all about,

So I reckon it's business as usual and only now and then does nervousness make me nauseous.

You and I both know what it's like to have other guys stepping on your head,

And you can't get on when you're dead.

TK.

So you think it's worth me giving it a shot?

MARYLOU.

Get out, TK, and give it all you've got.

After all, what happens if you fail?

TK.

I end up broke and in jail.

MARYLOU.

Look, with his own collapse Boesky did the biggest insider deal of all:

The SEC let him unload over a billion dollars worth of shares ahead of announcing his fall.

So paying a hundred million dollar fine was pretty minimal.

Which is great, because he overstepped some regulations, sure, but the guy's no criminal.

Like he said about his own amazing wealth.
'Greed is all right. Greed is healthy. You can be greedy and still feel good about yourself.'

Buy twenty million shares in Albion today.
(That's in addition to what you've bought.)
In a few weeks when Corman announces the bid and the price shoots up, we sell quick, take the profit, and on our way.

DUCKETT, *chairman of* ALBION, *and* MS BIDDULPH, *a white knight. Both from the north.*

DUCKETT.
Biddulph, I'm desperate. Corman's going to take over Albion. Shall I pay him greenmail and take on half a million debt? Shall I do one of those American things, poison pills, shark repellent, make some arrangement so the company comes to bits if he gets hold of it? Shall I cash in my Eurobond and emigrate?

BIDDULPH.
Now Duckett, you're under quite serious attack.
It's time to fight back.

DUCKETT.
I'd like to fight back.

BIDDULPH.
I know you'd give Corman a terrible fright
If you had a white knight.

DUCKETT.
I'd like a white knight.

BIDDULPH.
Now Corman will throw the top management out
But I'd guarantee that your job would remain.

DUCKETT.
Say it again?

BIDDULPH.
Your job would remain.
But Corman would throw the top management out.
That's what it's about.

DUCKETT.
That's what it's about.
But you'd guarantee that my job would remain.

BIDDULPH.
So if I should step in would I have your support?

DUCKETT.
Would you have my support!

BIDDULPH.
That's just what I thought.

DUCKETT.
It's very unfair to be attacked like this. I run a highly efficient company. I've sacked the finance director and the chief of marketing who'd both been with the company ten years. I've closed two factories and made five hundred people redundant. No one can say I'm not a hardhitting management.

BIDDULPH.
Hold on, Duckett, you've got it all wrong. Think of it from the PR angle. You're an old-fashioned firm. A good old English firm that has the loyalty of its employees and the support of the local community. You spend a lot of money on research and development.

DUCKETT.
I spend some, I suppose, but I always consider the shareholders' dividend and the short-term –

BIDDULPH.
No no no, you consider the long term. You're the kind of company the CBI likes. Corman means short-term profit. You mean industrial development. Think of Pilkington, Duckett. You're loved locally. Children like you. Dogs.

DUCKETT.
What I dream of you know is cornering the coffee market. Brazil needs to be hammered into the ground and the price kept right down low and –

BIDDULPH.
No, Duckett, not at the moment.

You're a sweet English maiden, all shining and bright.
And Corman's the villain intent upon rape
And I'm the white knight

DUCKETT.
You're the white knight

BIDDULPH.
And the knight has a fight and the maiden escapes
And when I'm in charge I'll put everything right.
(We can talk about closing Scunthorpe later.)

ZAC.

ZAC.

Jake couldn't have picked a worse time to die if he hated my guts.
Corman hadn't slept for forty-eight hours and was driving himself and everyone else nuts.
Jake was my one real friend over here. It's not that I don't care,
But the deal could get clinched today and I júst don't have the attention to spare.
(If he's put me in the shit with the DTI I'll worry about that later.)

ÇORMAN, ZAC, ETHERINGTON *and others of* CORMAN*'s team.*

CORMAN.

Right, you all know the position,
Biddulph's stepped in as a white knight to stop us making the acquisition.
Don't worry, she hasn't a chance, it's just a try on.
We've 15% of Albion stock plus 20% fan club holdings whose votes we can rely on.
Two aims:
One. Boost our own share price by getting anyone at all to buy Corman stock to increase the value of our offer. Two. Get anyone at all who'll vote for us to buy up Albion shares.
So in a word, get anyone you can by any means you can to buy both our stock and theirs.
From today we're coming to the crunch.
Nobody's going out any more to lunch.
(You can cancel dinner too.)
From today, we're going for the gold.
Put your family life and your sex life on hold.
A deal like this, at the start you gently woo it.
There comes a time when you get in there and screw it.
So you get the stock. And I don't care how you do it.

ETHERINGTON.

My reputation for integrity
Compels me to suggest you should take care.
No point succeeding if that same success
Destroys you and your company forever.
Remember Guinness.

CORMAN.

Thank you, Etherington. Some of us have work to do here.

ZAC.

There's no question there are thin lines and this is definitely a grey area.

And since Guinness it's a whole lot scarier.
You can't play ball if you keep off the grass.
So promise whatever you have to. Peddle your ass.
Let's give it all we've got and worry later.

CORMAN (*to* ETHERINGTON).
Are you standing there as some kind of arbitrator?
You can piss off, I'll get another broker.
The last thing I need in my pack is some tight-arsed joker.
(I thought you were good at this.)

ETHERINGTON.
My duty has been done in speaking out.
And now I'll help in every way I can.
My reputation for integrity
Will reassure our colleagues of their safety
In making any purchase we advise.

CORMAN.
Then let's get on / with it.

ZAC.
Let's get on with it, guys.

OTHERS *on phones.*

This works as a round, i.e. each starts at slash in previous speech and continues with all speeches as long as required. At end of each speech, each shouts out the amount of stock the person at the other end of the phone has agreed to buy, e.g. twenty thousand, a hundred thousand.

1. If you were interested in acquiring some Corman stock / there is a considerable sum on deposit with Klein Merrick so in the event of any subsequent fall in the share price you would be guaranteed against loss – 20,000
2. If you were interested in buying some Albion stock / there would be no question of being unable to dispose of them at a price at least equal to what you gave – 100,000
3. If you were able to see your way to supporting the bid / the new Albion under Corman management would naturally look favourably at any tenders for office cleaning that compared favourably with our present arrangements –
4. If you should be interested in following our recommendations to acquire Corman stock, an interest-free loan could be arranged at once with which the purchase could be made –

Meanwhile:

ZAC (*on phone*).
Remember me to Vanessa and the boys.
Listen, Corman, this may just be a rumour,
But if it's true it doesn't appeal to my sense of humour,
I've just had a word with a colleague in Atlanta & Gulf.
Marylou's been dealing with Biddulph.
I think it's time you spoke to her yourself.

CORMAN.
Dealing with Biddulph? I just sent her some flowers.
What the fuck does she think – ? She's meant to be one of ours.
I tried to call her this morning but I got the machine.
Leave a message after the tone? I'll leave something obscene.

CORMAN *phones* MARYLOU.

CORMAN.
Marylou? You got the flowers? A tragic bereavement.

MARYLOU.
Yes, TK made a real pretty arrangement.

CORMAN.
And our pretty arrangement's still OK?

MARYLOU.
I did dispose of a large holding today.

CORMAN.
You what? Disposed? A large Albion holding?
I gave you that on the clear understanding –

MARYLOU.
No, Corman, don't pursue it.
Anything I do I just happen to do because I want to do it.

CORMAN.
You owe me, Marylou.

MARYLOU.
I owe you?
I'm not even certain that I know you.

CORMAN.
How much Albion did you have?

MARYLOU.
15%.

CORMAN.
Can I just ask you where the hell it went?

MARYLOU.
Don't be slow, Bill. That's quite upsetting,
I like to think I'm dealing with an equal.

CORMAN.
Marylou, it's not that I'm not smart.
It's just hard to believe you'd break my heart.
Biddulph? Biddulph? what? you knew you were getting
Information from me / via Zackerman via Jake Todd.

MARYLOU.
You can't predict the sequel.

SCILLA *arrives unnoticed by* ZAC *or* CORMAN.

CORMAN.
But you knew Jake Todd was one of mine.

MARYLOU.
You are slow, / Bill.

CORMAN.
Because he's dead? you didn't want to be connected
With Jake now he's dead in case someone suspected – /
So that's why you sold to Biddulph.

MARYLOU.
I hope these phones are adequately scrambled.

CORMAN.
I don't give a fuck who else is on the line.
You cheated me. / I hate you. I'll fucking annihilate you.

MARYLOU.
Corman, you'll get rumbled
If you don't keep your temper. Be glad you're alive
(as my very irritating old aunty used to say).
Don't worry about it. What's 15%? Get after the other 85.

MARYLOU *hangs up*.

ZAC.
We need her.

Pause during which SCILLA *explains herself quietly to one of* CORMAN'*s team.*

SCILLA.
Kissogram for Mr Corman.

CORMAN *calls* MARYLOU *back*.

CORMAN.
Marylou? You know how it is. You say things in haste.
Our friendship's far too important / to waste

MARYLOU.
What do you want, Bill?

CORMAN.
Can you see your way to going back into Albion?
Will you buy Corman and support our price?
Smashing Biddulph would be very nice /
If you've anything –

MARYLOU.
Bill, I'd be glad to do something for you / but

CORMAN.
I understand your problem, how can I reassure you?

MARYLOU.
I'm playing with about a billion
But most of that's occupied over here.
If I had another hundred million
In my investment fund,
Then I guess / I'd have a freer hand.

CORMAN.
I think I can probably see my way clear.
This is hardly the moment with so much else on our minds.
But I had been meaning for some time to approach you with a view to becoming a contributor to your investment fund because I have of course the greatest admiration / for your wide experience and market timing.

MARYLOU.
I could have my people send you some documentation.

MARYLOU *hangs up*.

SCILLA *approaches* CORMAN *and sings*.

SCILLA.
Happy takeover day.
Take Albion away.
Happy takeover, Corman.
Happy takeover day.

CORMAN.
What the hell?

SCILLA.
Kissogram from Marylou Baines.

CORMAN.
From Marylou Baines? I'll kill her.

SCILLA.
I'm not really. I'm Jake Todd's sister, Scilla.

ZAC.
What the —

CORMAN.
What? Is this a terrorist a- /
ttack?

SCILLA.
I heard you. 'Jake Todd was one of mine.'
Tell me what it's all about. /
Did someone kill Jake?

CORMAN.
Will someone please get this lunatic out?

ZAC.
Hold it, hold it, everything's fine.
I know her, it's OK, she's not insane, she won't be armed, don't press
The security button, we'll be held up for hours with water sprinklers and the SAS. /
(Let's get on with the job here.)

SCILLA.
You killed my brother.

CORMAN.
Zac.

ZAC.
He didn't / he really didn't. I'm certain he didn't.

CORMAN.
Do you work for Marylou Baines?
(Because you can tell her from me –)

SCILLA.
No, that was a trick to get in. / Now will you explain

CORMAN.
(Don't work for her.)

SCILLA.
what 'one of mine' means. One of your what?
He did something illegal. You were frightened of what he'd say
To the DTI and you wanted him out of the way.
Tell me what's going on or I'll tell the press
My brother was acting for you the night he was shot.
Did you kill him yourself or get your broker to pull the trigger?

CORMAN.
After the deal, after the deal I'll confess
To murdering anyone just let me get on with the deal.

SCILLA.
You and Zac got Jake into some mess.
He did little fiddles but this must have been much bigger.
You and Zac got him involved in some corrupt / ring

CORMAN.
Suppose I had killed Jake, his ghost would have had more sense than walk in here today and interrupt. /

ZAC.
Can you spare me for five minutes?

CORMAN.
He got on because he knew what was a priority / and he'd have reckoned

SCILLA.
He got on. Doing what exactly?

CORMAN.
That matters of life and death came a poor second.

ZAC.
Can you spare me for five minutes?

CORMAN.
No, not for two. / Go on.

SCILLA.
I'm not leaving here / until you –

ZAC.
I'll tell you. / I'll tell you.

SCILLA.
You will.

CORMAN.
You'll what?

ZAC.
Can I handle this? Can I just handle this please?

ZAC *and* SCILLA *outside* CORMAN'*s office.*

SCILLA.
So tell me.

ZAC.
Marylou Baines – we'll make it quick, OK? /
Needs inside information and she's willing to pay.

SCILLA.
You knew all this this morning and you didn't say.

ZAC.
So anyone in London with news would give it to Jake,
And he'd get half a percent / on whatever she'd make.

SCILLA.
Half a percent?
That meant . . .

ZAC.
If she made fifty million –

SCILLA.
He got two hundred and fifty thousand.
If she made two hundred million / – he never told me.

ZAC.
I think little Jakey could have bought and sold me.
So now you know, OK? And now you drop it.

SCILLA.
What do you mean? / I'm just getting started.

ZAC.
I've got work to do.

CORMAN.
Who killed him? Corman? You?

ZAC.
I'm too tenderhearted
And Corman's too busy. Scilla, stop it.
We have to keep this quiet now. Face the facts.
You're never going to find out all Jake's contacts.
Let it go. I've got work to do. Don't get in a state.

SCILLA.
You knew all along. He never told me. Wait.

ZAC *goes*.

He was making serious money.

So Zac went back to Corman and I thought I'd better go to work despite Jake being dead because Chicago comes in at one twenty and I hate to miss it. I work on the floor of Liffe, the London International Financial Futures Exchange.

Trading options and futures looks tricky if you don't understand it.
But if you're good at market timing you can make out like a bandit.
(It's the most fun I've had since playing cops and robbers with Jake when we were children.)
A simple way of looking at futures is take a commodity,
Coffee, cocoa, sugar, zinc, pork bellies, copper, aluminium, oil –

I always think pork bellies is an oddity.
(They could just as well have a future in chicken wings.)
Suppose you're a coffee trader and there's a drought in Brazil like last year or suppose there's a good harvest, either way you might lose out,
So you can buy a futures contract that works in the opposite direction so you're covered against loss, and that's what futures are basically about.
But of course you don't have to take delivery of anything at all.
You can buy and sell futures contracts without any danger of ending up with ten tons of pork bellies in the hall.
On the floor of Liffe the commodity is money.
You can buy and sell money, you can buy and sell absence of money, debt, which used to strike me as funny.
For some it's hedging, for most it's speculation.
In New York they've just introduced a futures contract in inflation.
(Pity it's not Bolivian inflation, which hit forty thousand per cent.)
I was terrified when I started because there aren't many girls and they line up to watch you walk,
And every time I opened my mouth I felt self-conscious because of the way I talk.
I found O levels weren't much use, the best qualified people are street traders.
But I love it because it's like playing a cross between roulette and space invaders.

LIFFE canteen.

SCILLA. JOANNE *a runner*. KATHY *a trader*.

JOANNE.
I said I'm not going to work down there.
It's like animals in a zoo. / So then I thought I'll have a bash.

KATHY.
When you start they really stare.

SCILLA.
Don't let them see you care.

JOANNE.
I'll never learn what to do. / I'll never learn hand signals.

SCILLA.
I couldn't walk across the floor / my first day.

KATHY.
This morning's really a bore, / there's nothing happening.

JOANNE.
I answered a telephone / for the first time.
KATHY.
You really feel on your own.
SCILLA.
Never say hold on / because they don't hold on.
KATHY.
I can manage two phones at once but not three.
SCILLA.
Sometimes I've put the phone down because I don't know what they're saying.
JOANNE.
You do get used to the noise. I nearly fainted the first day.
KATHY.
I can deal without shouting, most of them like shouting.
SCILLA.
Men are just little boys. / Dave had lost twenty slips at the end of yesterday and muggins finds them for him.
JOANNE.
Terry asked me out this morning. He was the first person who spoke to me on my first day, he was really friendly.
Is it all right going out? / Do they talk about you?
SCILLA.
You do get talked about, / I hear so and so's knocking off so and so.
KATHY.
Just go out for lunch, / then nothing can happen after.
SCILLA.
They're a very chauvinist bunch.
KATHY.
We've all been out with Terry.
SCILLA.
Anyway they're all too knackered / by the end of the day.
KATHY.
It's true, they're all frustrated / because they never have time to do it.
JOANNE.
I'm completely exhausted.
At midnight I'm washing my knickers / because I'm too speedy to sleep.

KATHY.
I get up at half-past five and have a good breakfast.

SCILLA.
Mind you, I like Terry.

TERRY, DAVE, MARTIN, BRIAN *and* VINCE, *traders, arrive.*

KATHY.
Hello, Terry.

TERRY.
What about Saturday?

JOANNE.
I don't know.

TERRY.
Think about it.

KATHY.
Better be getting back.

MARTIN.
Time we did some work. Nearly time for Chicago.

VINCE.
Coming out with me tonight?

SCILLA.
Leave it out, Vince.

DAVE.
Leave the lady alone.

VINCE (*to* JOANNE).
Coming out with me tonight?

KATHY.
Leave it out, Vince.

Floor of LIFFE. Four separate companies each with their phones, and a trading pit.
Klein Merrick has SCILLA *on the phone,* TERRY *and* DAVE *on the floor,* MANDY *as runner.*
2 – has SHERILL *on the phone,* MARTIN *and* KATHY *on the floor,* PETE *as runner.*
3 – has DICK *on the phone,* BRIAN *and* JILL *on the floor,* JOANNE *as runner.*
4 – has MARY *on the phone,* VINCE *and* JOHN *on the floor,* ANNIE *as runner.*
They all start going to their places. As ANNIE, *who is new, walks down the lads cheer and jeer.*

TERRY.
You're in late.

SCILLA.
Trouble at home. My brother's been shot.

TERRY.
You what?

SCILLA.
There's going to be a scandal.

TERRY.
Another one? / Did you say your brother?

SCILLA.
Bigger.

TERRY.
Is it worth trading on?

SCILLA.
There might be a run on sterling if you're lucky.

KATHY.
Ere come the c'nardlies.

BRIAN.
Fuck off, sweaty git.

DICK.
Fuck off, dogbreath.

BRIAN.
Yeh, lovely. I'll feel better when I get rid of these oysters.

SCILLA.
Dave! Dave!

BRIAN.
And how are you this morning?

JILL.
Don't talk to me, I'm all fucked up.

JOANNE.
Do you call him Dick because he's got spots?

JILL.
No, I call him Spot because he's a dick.

VINCE.
Annie, if you sell the front and buy the back, / you'll be short of front and long of back.

BRIAN.
Muff city, no pity.

SCILLA.
Dave, Grimes says Zac's got a ten million rollover for March so sell 10 at 9. If you can't get it he'll go to 8. And 15 June at your best price.

TERRY.
Are you Annie? Can you find this guy and give him a message?

ANNIE.
Mike who?

TERRY.
Hunt.

KATHY.
I'm tired of making money for other people. I'd like to be a local.

SCILLA.
Oi! Dave! You can't signal with a pencil in your hand.

DAVE.
Just fuckin have, haven't I.

KATHY.
The theoretical spread is too large.[1]

JOANNE.
Did you see that actor from *The Bill* who was in here yesterday?

KATHY.
I saw him first.

JOANNE.
I saw him first.

KATHY.
I wonder if he'll come back.

JOANNE.
I wonder if he's married.

Trading is now getting going.

JOANNE.
What do you want this morning?

PETE.
She wants 18 at 15.

JOANNE.
All I want is a bacon roll.

PETE (*sings*).
All I want is a bacon roll.

Meanwhile:

DAVE.
[1]Red June is showing 4 bid for 5.
TERRY.
Sterling showing 5 at 3.
DICK (*phone*).
March showing 9.
(*To* BRIAN *on floor*.) 5 at 9. 5 at 9.
(*Another phone call*.) Is that another 5 or the same 5?
(*To* BRIAN.) 5 more at 9. 5 more. 10 at 9. 10 at 9.
BRIAN.
5 at 9 filled.[2]
DICK (*phone*).
Your first 5 at 9 filled.
SHERILL.
We want 20 out of Footsie and into gilts.[3]
(*To* MARTIN.) Sell 20 at 1. 20 at 1.
(*To* KATHY.) Bid 9 for 20, 9 for 20.
MARTIN.
20 at 1.
KATHY.
9 for 20.
MARY.
[2]March gilts 8 rising fast. Do you want to sell now or wait? They might go another two ticks if you're lucky. (*To floor*.) 5 at 9. 5 at 9.
BRIAN.
[3]Where we going tonight?
TERRY.
The old Chinese?
BRIAN.
Dragon city, no pity.
DAVE.
I'll tell Vince.
BRIAN.
Oi, we're 18 for 15.
TERRY.
18 for 15. Working 20.
DAVE.
Table for 15 please.
JOHN.
10 at 19. 10 at 19.

VINCE.
John John John – just 5 at 19.
You can't trust John's bids.

MARY.
He's had too many beers.

DAVE.
I've got a certain winner for the 3.30 if anyone's interested.[4]

BRIAN.
You haven't paid us yesterday's winnings yet.

DAVE.
Leave it out, Brian, I always pay you.

KATHY.
[4]Come on gilts. 2 at 4 the gilts.

MARTIN.
Sterling showing 5 at 3.

TERRY.
Euro 4 bid now.

SCILLA.
Dave, you're supposed to be looking at me right?

DAVE.
Am I in or am I out?[5]

MANDY.
You gotta listen. If you don't listen we can't get in touch with you.

DAVE.
What?

SCILLA.
If you look at me I won't give you stick.

VINCE.
[5]10 bid for 70. Let's get some stock away.

MARTIN.
Where the fuck have you been?

PETE.
Oh I see, you're not even allowed to crap.

MARTIN.
If Tony rings tell him I can't get out.

BRIAN.
I'm long on Footsie.

DAVE.
Don't know why I bothered coming in today.

MARTIN.
It's really flying. / It's really going somewhere.

SCILLA (*to* MANDY).
Find out if Brian bought 20 off Dave at 6.

MANDY *goes to* BRIAN.

MANDY.
Did you buy 20 off Dave at 6?[6]

BRIAN.
Going to the Greenhouse tonight?

DICK (*to* BRIAN).
[6]5 at 9. Have you got that second 5 at 9 filled?

JILL (*to* BRIAN).
Have you got that second 5 at 9 filled?

BRIAN.
Leave me alone, I'm talking to the young lady.[7]

ANNIE *comes up to* BRIAN.

ANNIE.
I'm looking for Mike Hunt.

BRIAN.
She's looking for her cunt.

ANNIE *realises and starts to cry.* MANDY *takes her back to her trading booth.*

MANDY.
Don't worry, they do it to everyone when they're new.

SHERILL.
OUT OUT OUT!
[7]John, phone for you.

MARTIN.
My car keeps getting stolen.

SAM.
Don't leave it outside your house.

PETE.
Then they won't know it's yours.

VINCE.
Terry! It's a doddle, four-hour drive at most.

TERRY.
It's four hundred, five, it's five hundred miles.

BRIAN.
I'm not doing that / on a Sunday.

DICK.
Check your oil the night before and leave at five.

TERRY.
What's he doing living in a castle?

VINCE.
He's a fucking iron.

ALL FOUR.
Iron 'oof! /

SCILLA.
Chicago two minutes. Footsie's going to move.

DAVE.
No, he showed me a picture of his girlfriend once with a carrot in her mouth right up to the green bit.

BRIAN.
Veg city, no pity.

JOHN.
Dave, the horse! It won!

DAVE *and* JOHN *embrace and jump up and down.*

DAVE.
I fucking won two thousand pounds!

KATHY.
Chicago, Chicago.

Everyone is suddenly quiet, watching the boards, waiting for Chicago to come in. All burst out at once, furious trading, everyone flat out. Among the things we hear:

VINCE.
6 for 10. 6 for 10.

JOHN.
10 at 6. 10 at 6.

VINCE.
I'm buying at 6, you cunt.

SHERILL (*on phone*).
11 coming 10, 11 coming 10, 11 10 11 10, 10! 10 10 10 10 coming 9, 10 coming 9, etc.

BRIAN.
What's your fucking game?

MARTIN.
Oh fuck off.

BRIAN.
I'll fucking break your leg, you fucking cunt.

SCILLA (*to* DAVE).
You'll have to shout louder if you can't signal better.

BRIAN (*to* DAVE). You're trading like a cunt.

Out of furious trading emerges the song:

FUTURES SONG

Out you cunt, out in oh fuck it
I've dealt the gelt below the belt and I'm jacking up the ackers
My front's gone short, fuck off old sport, you're standing on my knackers
I've spilt my guts, long gilt's gone nuts and I think I'm going crackers
So full of poo I couldn't screw, I fucked it with my backers
I fucked it with my backers
I fucked it with my backers

Backups: Out! Buy buy buy! Leave it!
No! Yes! Cunt!
4! 5! Sell!
Quick! Prick! Yes! No! Cunt!

How hard I dredge to earn my wedge, I'm sharper than a knife
Don't fucking cry get out and buy, Chicago's going rife
You're back to front come on you cunt don't give me any strife
You in or out? Don't hang about, you're on the floor of Liffe!

They call me a tart who can hardly fart when it's bedlam in the pit
I'm the local tootsie playing footsie but I don't mind a bit
Cos my future trusts my money lusts as far as it can spit
And my sterling works on mouthy jerks whose bids are full of shit

I'm a Romford scholar in eurodollars and June is showing four
Botham out nineteen on the Reuters screen is the very latest score
I fucked that runner she's a right little stunner so I pulled her off the floor
I was bidding straight till my interest rate jumped up and asked for more

Money-making money-making money-making money-making
Money-making money-making money-making caper
Do the fucking business do the fucking business do the fucking business
And bang it down on paper.

So L.I.F.F.E. is the life for me and I'll burn out when I'm dead
And this fair exchange is like a rifle range what's the price of flying lead?
When you soil your jeans on soya beans shove some cocoa up your head
You can never hide if your spread's too wide, you'll just fuck yourself instead.

ACT TWO

JACINTA CONDOR *flying first class.*

JACINTA.

Flight to England that little grey island in the clouds where governments don't fall overnight and children don't sell themselves in the street and my money is safe. I'll buy a raincoat. I'll meet Jake Todd, I'll stay at the Savoy by the stream they call a river with its Bloody Tower and dead queens, a river is too wide to bridge. The unfinished bridge across the canyon where the road ends in the air, waiting for dollars. The office blocks father started, imagining glass, leather, green screens, the city rising high into the sky, but the towers stopped short, cement, wires, the city spreading wider instead with a blur of shacks, miners coming down from the mountains as the mines close. The International Tin Council, what a scandal, thank God I wasn't in tin, the price of copper ruined by the frozen exchange rate, the two rates, and the government will not let us mining companies exchange enough dollars at the better rate, they insist we help the country in this crisis, I do not want to help, I want to be rich, I close my mines and sell my copper on the London Metal Exchange. It is all because of the debt that will never be paid because we have to borrow more and more to pay the interest on the money that came from oil when OPEC had too much money and your western banks wanted to lend it to us because who else would pay such high interest, needing it so badly? Father got his hands on enough of it but what happened, massive inflation, lucky he'd put the money somewhere safe, the Swiss mountains so white from the air like our mountains but the people rich with cattle and clocks and secrets, the American plains yellow with wheat, the green English fields where lords still live in grey stone, all with such safe banks and good bonds and exciting gambles, so as soon as any dollars or pounds come, don't let them go into our mines or our coffee or look for a sea of oil under the jungle, no get it out quickly to the western banks (a little money in cocaine, that's different). Peru leads the way resisting the IMF, refusing to pay the interest, but I don't want to make things difficult for the banks, I prefer to support them, why should my money stay in Peru and suffer? The official closing price yesterday for grade A copper was 878-8.5, three months 900.5–1, final kerb close 901-2. Why bother to send aid so many miles, put it straight into my eurobonds.

Meanwhile the London metal exchange starts quietly trading copper. When JACINTA *finishes speaking the trading reaches its noisy climax.*

ZAC.

There's some enterprising guys around and here's an example.
You know how if you want to get a job in the States you have to give a urine sample?
(this is to show you're not on drugs).
There's a company now for a fifty dollar fee
They'll provide you with a guaranteed pure, donated by a churchgoer, bottle of pee.
(They also plan to market it dehydrated in a packet and you just add water.)
And Aids is making advertisers perplexed
Because it's no longer too good to have your product associated with sex.
But it's a great marketing opportunity.
Like the guys opening up blood banks where you pay to store your own blood in case of an accident and so be guaranteed immunity.
(It's also a great time to buy into rubber.)
Anyone who can buy oranges for ten and sell at eleven in a souk or bazaar
Has the same human nature and can go equally far.
The so-called third world doesn't want our charity or aid.
All they need is the chance to sit down in front of some green screens and trade.
(They don't have the money, sure, but just so long as they have freedom from communism so they can do it when they do have the money.)
Pictures of starving babies are misleading and patronising.
Because there's plenty of rich people in those countries, it's just the masses that's poor, and Jacinta Condor flew into London and was quite enterprising.
It was the day before Jake Todd was found dead
And the deal was really coming to a head.
Jake was helping us find punters because anyone with too much money and Jake would know them.
You'd just say, Jake, who's in town, what have you got, and he'd bring them in and show them.

ZAC *and* JAKE.

JAKE.
Señora Condor has plenty of cash in her coffer.
She owns mountains and her garden's twice
The size of Wales. What's Corman going to offer?

ZAC.
He hopes she'll be able to help support his price.

JAKE.
She's going to need some kind of incentive.

ZAC.
I think she'll find Corman quite inventive.

JAKE.
Zac, while we're alone.
I didn't want to say this on the phone.
I had a visit from a DTI inspector.

ZAC.
Have you done something not quite correct or / what?

JAKE.
Zac, it's no joke. They didn't say too much /
But once they –

ZAC.
Did they mention me?

JAKE.
I can't say I don't know
You. / (That doesn't tell them anything, knowing you.)

ZAC.
Great.
Sure, no, of course not.

JAKE.
Don't let's pay too much
Attention to it. OK? / If you like I'll go.

ZAC.
It could be quite a smash. /
Not just for you.

JAKE.
I have been making quite a lot of cash.
When they take your passport you feel surprisingly trapped.
I didn't know I was so fond of travel.

ZAC.
You're the kind of loose thread, Jake, that when they pull you the whole fucking City could unravel.

JAKE.
Shall we cancel Condor in case it makes things worse?

ZAC.
Just don't give them the whole thing giftwrapped.

JAKE.
I can walk out the door now.

ZAC.
OK.

JAKE.
I feel –

JAKE.
What shall I do?

ZAC.
Jake, I'm not your nurse.

JAKE.
Tell me to walk / and I'll walk.

ZAC.
And fuck up the deal?

JAKE.
There might be a bug on the light.

ZAC.
Jake, what the hell.
There might be a microphone under your lapel.
The City's greed or fear, you've got to choose.

JAKE.
Greed's been good to me. Fear's a bitch.

ZAC.
Then be greedy, guy, and let's get this payload home without a hitch.

JAKE.
I can always hit the straight and narrow tomorrow.

JACINTA CONDOR *arrives.*

This is Zac Zackerman you've heard so much about.
The guy who always knows the latest shout.

ZAC.
How are you enjoying your stay in London, Señora Condor?

JACINTA.
I have been for a walk
In your little saint's park

Where the pelicans eat the pigeons (but I didn't see it).
I have been to the opera (very nice).
I have sold all my copper
For a rather small number of millions.

ZAC.
This is no time to sell copper, the price is lousy.

JAKE.
And when's it ever in season?
She's selling copper she's got to have a reason.

JACINTA.
I lose every quarter,
The cash goes like water,
Is better to close the mine.
I chose very well
The moment to sell,
I benefit from the closures in Surinam because of guerrilla activity and also I leak the news I am closing my mines, which puts the price up a little, so it is fine.

JAKE.
So you've wiped out your mines? That's telling them who's master.
You must feel like a natural disaster.

ZAC.
Hurricane Jacinta.

JACINTA.
If I keep them Jake I have to be derange.
The Minister of Energy says 'Mining is not dead' –
It brings 45% of our foreign exchange
But a pound of copper won't buy a loaf of bread.
(Our mining companies lost a hundred million dollars last year, it is the fault of IMF. I don't like to suffer.)

JAKE.
The dagos always like to blame the gringos.
I suppose the miners want a revolution.
The most amazing lake full of flamingos –
(I think that was Peru.)

JACINTA.
How can I support ten thousand people?
When I did they weren't even grateful.
The miners all strike
And do what they like,
They want subsidised food, I say get on your bike.

JAKE.
I didn't know they had bikes, I thought they had llamas, /
And woolly hats and trousers like pyjamas.

ZAC.
(So are the miners bothering you?

JACINTA.
You come and protect me?)
It's really a pity,
They go to the city (where there's no work)
Or they sit down outside the mine.
Growing coca is nice,
A very good price
(Ten to thirty times as much as tea or coffee or cocoa)
So I think that's going to be fine.

JAKE.
Great product to grow.
Peru with its mountains covered in snow.
You're not giving up all your Peruvian interests?

JACINTA.
Europe is more interesting. Mr Corman is fascinating.
Jake, I have asked a friend to this meeting.

ZAC.
I'm not sure a –

JACINTA.
You've heard of Nigel Ajibala?

ZAC.
I can't say I have.

JAKE.
Listen, don't cross the señora.

JACINTA.
I tell you I've caught a
Big cocoa importer,
Your deal goes without a hitch.
His school was at Eton
Where children are beaten,
He's a prince and exceedingly rich.

JAKE.
Any friend of Jacinta
Will be a good punter.

ZAC.
So where does he operate?

JACINTA.
He has connections in
Ghana and Zambia
Zaire and Gambia
But it's here that he likes to invest.
His enemies are jealous
Because he's so zealous (and makes so much money) /
And at home he faces arrest
(like the man they tried to kidnap in the trunk?)

JAKE.
You see, I told you, it's great.

JACINTA.
Here he comes now. Be cunning.

ZAC.
I suppose Corman can always meet him.

NIGEL AJIBALA *arrives.*

JACINTA.
My friend, Jake Todd, and Mr Zackerman,
A very considerable American.

JAKE.
You spend much time in Zambia and Zaire?

NIGEL.
Yes, but one's mostly based over here.
Africa induces mild hysteria.
Terrible situation in Nigeria.
(oil earnings down from twenty-five billion dollars to five this year so they're refusing to make their interest payments.)
And Zaire
Pays the west a hundred and ninety million more than it receives each year.
So as the last of several last resorts
It's cutting its payments to 10% of exports.

JACINTA.
So the IMF
Will turn a deaf
Ear.

NIGEL.
They've just cut off their payments to Zambia.

ZAC.
The IMF is not a charity.
It has to insist on absolute austerity.

NIGEL.
Absolutely. It can't be namby pamby.
These countries must accept restricted diets.
The governments must explain, if there are food riots,
That paying the western banks is the priority.

JAKE.
Bob Geldof was a silly cunt.
He did his charity back to front.
They should have had the concerts in Zaire
And shipped the money to banks over here.

ZAC.
So you're better off out of Africa, I guess.

NIGEL.
The continent is such a frightful mess.
One's based in London so one's operation
Is on the right side of exploitation.
One thing one learned from one's colonial masters,
One makes money from other people's disasters.

ZAC.
Señora Condor tells me you might be interested in Corman Enterprise.

ZAC *takes* NIGEL *aside.*

JAKE.
You can't completely pull out of Peru.

JACINTA.
Don't worry, Jake, I don't pull out on you.
I give up all my interests – except the cocaine.
And I keep the houses of course and the aeroplane.
My country is beautiful, Jake, white mountains, jungle greenery.
My people will starve to death among the scenery.
(Let them rot. I'm sick of it.)

JAKE.
So what's the story?

JACINTA.
The airstrip's rebuilt –
The government feels guilt
So it's always trying to bomb it.
(also they try to destroy my processing plants which is deceitful because they dare not confront the peasants and stop them growing it.)
And they don't really want
To destroy all the plants.

They are making billions from it (more than all the rest of our exports).
To keep Reagan our friend
We have to pretend,
But the US pretends and we know it.
Who likes a coke buzz?
America does.
They stop using it, we won't grow it.

JAKE.
So when can we see some action? Let's get going.

JACINTA.
I have to get a little cash flowing.
Maybe Mr Corman?

JAKE.
I'm curious to see Corman, we've never met,
I'm just a secret compartment in his desk.
He's very bright so be on your best behaviour.
He's obsessed with the bid and he'll look on you as a saviour.
You can push him quite hard, he likes a risk.
So have you decided what to ask for yet?

JACINTA.
If I buy or sell
I always do well
So don't worry about it, my pet.
Whatever I get
I look after you
And Corman will too
I expect.
Don't be embarrassed, Jake, you're young and greedy, I like to see it.

ZAC *and* NIGEL *rejoin them.*

JAKE.
I was at Eton myself. This is rather a different ballgame.

NIGEL.
Oh not at all. Did you ever play the wall game?

JAKE *and* NIGEL *talk apart.*

ZAC.
It would be great to see you while you're over here.

JACINTA.
Maybe we could drink some English beer.
I have a meeting at eight,

It won't go on late.
Maybe at half-past nine?

ZAC.
No, I don't think . . .
I'll be stuck with Corman, I can't get out for a drink.
Eleven's probably fine.

JACINTA.
I'm having late supper
With terribly upper-
class people who buy my plantation.

ZAC.
And after that?

JACINTA.
Unfortunately they live in Edinburgh.

ZAC.
How you getting there?

JACINTA.
By helicopter.

ZAC.
I'm beginning to run out of inspiration.

JACINTA.
Breakfast?

ZAC.
Would be great except I have to have breakfast with Corman till this deal goes through.
I suppose I might get away for a minute or two.

JACINTA.
That would be heaven.

ZAC.
Maybe eleven?

JACINTA.
Eleven I see my lawyer.
At twelve –

ZAC.
No, please.

JACINTA.
I see some Japanese,
Just briefly in the hotel foyer.
So we meet for lunch?

ZAC.
I have to be in Paris for lunch. I'll be back by four.
JACINTA.
That's good!
ZAC.
But I have to go straight to Corman.
JACINTA.
What a bore.
ZAC.
Maybe we could . . .
JACINTA.
Dinner tomorrow
Much to my sorrow
I have with some eurobond dealers.
ZAC.
Cancel it.
JACINTA.
Business.
ZAC.
Shit.
JACINTA.
Afterward?
ZAC.
Bliss.
No, hang on a minute.
I have as a guest a
Major investor,
I have to put out some feelers.
(The only time he can meet me is after a show.)
I guess I might be through by 1 a.m.
JACINTA.
Zac, I could cry,
There's a nightclub I buy,
And really I must talk to them.
So maybe next morning
You give me a ring?
ZAC.
Maybe I can get out of breakfast with Corman, I'll call you first thing.
JACINTA.
Which day?

ZAC.
Tomorrow.

NIGEL *and* JAKE.

NIGEL.
If you fancy a wolfhound I'll let you have a pup.

JAKE.
If I'm down in Wiltshire I'll certainly look you up.

ZAC *takes* JAKE *aside*.

JACINTA (*to* NIGEL).
That went very well.
They can't possibly tell
You live in one room in a rundown hotel.
I'll buy you a silk shirt in Jermyn Street.

ZAC *and* JAKE.

ZAC.
You've not met Corman before, had you better split?
There may be a good time to meet him but is this it?
If you've actually spoken it gets us in more deep –

JAKE.
What the hell, Zac. Hang for a sheep.

ZAC *joins* CORMAN *and* ETHERINGTON *in* CORMAN'*s office*.

CORMAN.
Cup of coffee someone. I'm going mental.
So we get these people involved in distribution,
Or supply, whatever, and they make a contribution?

ZAC.
Their involvement should look kind of coincidental.

CORMAN.
Look what? Zac, don't you start talking sin,
It'll look terrific. Show the buggers in.

NIGEL, JACINTA *and* JAKE *come into* CORMAN'*s office*.

ZAC.
Señora Condor. Mr Ajibala.

CORMAN.
And this must be the infamous Jake Todd.
I'd begun to think you were a bit like God –
You make things happen but you don't exist.
Etherington, don't look as if you smell something burning.
This is Jake Todd, our invisible earning.

ETHERINGTON.
How do you do, Mr Todd. Extremely glad.

JAKE.
You're really so looked up to by my dad.

CORMAN.
OK, let's skip the introductions.
How do you do. Let's get on with the ructions.
What's the idea?

NIGEL.
Albion seems an excellent investment
Especially under your expert control.
I assure you that the stag is not my role.
I'm talking about a long term commitment.

CORMAN.
So you'd have the company's interests at heart?

NIGEL.
I'd certainly be glad to play my part.
I can't imagine why anyone bothers with water
When Albion produces so many delicious drinks.
Orange, coffee, chocolate / with cream –

CORMAN.
I think the product stinks.
Cocoa? you're a cocoa importer?
I know fuckall about the cocoa bean.
Buy the company first and run it later.

NIGEL.
The London market suits the speculator.
You really have to know your way around.
And excellent bargains can be made.

CORMAN.
You've wide experience have you in the trade?

NIGEL.
The only job I haven't done is peasant
Who grows the stuff, which wouldn't be so pleasant.

CORMAN.
So what's the story with cocoa –
Anyone know?
Are Albion having to pay through the nose?

NIGEL.
There's mistrust between the countries where it grows
And countries like this where we consume.

Cocoa is very far from having a boom.
A new agreement has just been implemented.

ZAC.
(Hell of a lot of wrangling about the buffer stock.)

NIGEL.
This has driven the price up a little but it's well below the price at which buffer stock buying is permitted,
And 18% down on a year ago.
We consumers are holding the price low.

CORMAN.
So how can you give me a better price than your rivals?

NIGEL.
Because options and futures are more important than physicals.
(In today's market following an unchanged opening futures rallied £15 during the afternoon before trade profit taking pared the gains on the closing call. With producers withdrawn physical interest was restricted to forward/consumer offtake –)

JAKE.
He buys a forward contract, sells it later,
And every time he's making money off it.

ZAC.
And you get the benefit of the profit.

JACINTA.
It's thrilling to watch such a skilful operator.

CORMAN.
And funny business with import licences, Mr Ajibala? Don't answer that.
Right Zac, let's put cocoa on the back burner.
It looks as if it's a nice little earner.
And you Señora? Are you full of beans?
I suppose you want to sell me some caffeine?

JACINTA.
Coffee's no joke,
It makes me go broke,
No, my interest is distribution –

CORMAN.
I spent a good weekend once in Caracas.
You don't by any chance play the maracas?

JACINTA.
I'm here to do business, Mr Corman.
I wish to obtain an exclusive franchise.

CORMAN.
Señoritas in Brazil have beautiful eyes.

ZAC.
Cut it out, Corman.

JACINTA.
Mr Corman, you appreciate my country's spirit.
I appreciate your company's products and I wish to sell it in Peru, Brazil, Argentina, Venezuela and Chile.

ZAC.
This could very probably be arranged.

CORMAN.
Zackerman, I hope you haven't changed.

ZAC.
The proposal has considerable merit.

CORMAN.
You wouldn't be suggesting something silly?
Can't you tell me anything good the present distributors did?

ZAC.
No, they've shown no interest at all in your bid.

CORMAN.
That's too bad.
I think we may be in business, Señora.

JACINTA.
If you want to set up
Debt for equity swap
And have Albion plants in Peru
It's a way that we get
To sell some of our debt.
I ask you, what else can we do?
Better than selling copper.

CORMAN.
Zac, do I want to invest in South America?

ZAC.
South American companies will swap their debt
For dollars you invest in their country, which means you get
Say a hundred million dollars of equity
Paid by the government in local currency
And you've only got to hand over seventy.
It gives you a great advantage over the locals.

JACINTA.
Also you could help to build my hospitals.
I have one for sick and hungry men and women,
One for poor drug-addicted children.
I visit and hold the hands of the poor people.

CORMAN.
This is all extremely admirable,
Don't you think so, Etherington? (*To* JACINTA.) If you'll excuse us.

CORMAN *takes* ZAC *and* ETHERINGTON *aside*.

Is this wise?
Hospitals, she's simply trying to use us.
Every penny would go in her own pocket.
Everything she looks at I want to lock it.
You can't help admiring the way she tries.
Etherington?

ETHERINGTON.
I'm afraid I can't advise.
Questions of supply and distribution
For Albion after you make the acquisition
Are matters of internal management,
So naturally, I haven't liked to listen. /
I really don't feel qualified to comment.

CORMAN.
Do you want the money for the deal or not?
Zac?

ZAC.
Swapping debt might come in handy later.
I agree the hospitals / are just a scam.

CORMAN.
Hospitals! what does she think I am?

ZAC.
So we buy his cocoa, give her the franchise and get out the calculator.

CORMAN.
They have got serious money?

ZAC.
Jake recommends / them.

CORMAN.
That boy's got very interesting friends.
Let's keep them sweet.

CORMAN *returns to others.*

I'd be delighted to make a small contribution
To your hospital, Señora. The distribution
Franchise would of course be contingent
On my acquiring Albion.

JACINTA.
I know the arrangement.
If you get it, I get it. I help you get it.

CORMAN.
And Mr Ajibala.
I'm most impressed. As Albion's sole supplier /
Of cocoa?

NIGEL.
I would feel it my duty to acquire /
An interest in the company.

CORMAN.
I think a change of supplier is probably indicated,
Don't you, Zac?
Right, you can both discuss the exact sum
With my banker here, Mr Zackerman.

NIGEL.
There's a small problem.
I was hoping to buy five-million poundsworth of Albion stock but I have a holdup in cash liquidity.

CORMAN.
That is a problem.

NIGEL.
I suppose it is a matter of some urgency?
If my involvement could be postponed, ten days, or eight?

CORMAN.
That's too late.

NIGEL.
If I had an extra two million now a five million purchase could be made by several small companies under various names registered in various places not traceable to anyone alive.

ZAC.
Maybe if he buys three million now / and two –

CORMAN.
Zac, I want five. Five!

NIGEL.
I don't have five at my immediate disposal.

CORMAN.
Mr Ajibala, if you're happy with my proposal / about the cocoa

NIGEL.
Perfectly.

CORMAN.
I could make a downpayment of two million in advance.
(We're going to need a hell of a lot of cocoa beans.)

NIGEL.
That way nothing would be left to chance.

CORMAN.
Zackerman will write a cheque.
And Señora Condor, if you see my lawyer.

JACINTA.
The deal is exciting,
I get it in writing?

CORMAN.
I can't be bothered with all these trivialities.
We've got the money. Fuck the personalities.
Etherington will see you all right for stock.

CORMAN *and* ETHERINGTON *leave, followed by* ZAC.

ZAC (*to* JACINTA).
I'll call you first thing.

JACINTA, NIGEL *and* JAKE *alone.*

NIGEL.
I've got the money! / Two million!

JACINTA.
For Albion?

NIGEL.
I want a better return,
Albion won't earn,

JACINTA.
Put up your stake,
Get it doubled / by Jake.

NIGEL.
Doubled?

JACINTA.
He's a good dealer, let him play with it.

JAKE.
No problem. Give me a week.

NIGEL.
I'll go and get the cheque from Zackerman.

NIGEL *goes.*

JACINTA.
Two million? What are you going to do?

JAKE.
I thought I might invest it in Peru.

JACINTA *phones* MARYLOU BAINES.

JACINTA.
Hello? Marylou?
Four million, repeat four,
Arrives Thursday, the usual way.

MARYLOU.
But the CIA
Won't help it through
Unless we agree to give /
another 10% to the Contras.

JACINTA.
But Marylou, already we pay –

MARYLOU.
I don't think we have an alternative.

JACINTA.
I expect an increase in what I get from you.

MARYLOU.
No problem. The guys who use it can easily meet
A rise in the street price because the street is Wall Street.

JACINTA.
So how's the weather?

MARYLOU.
I haven't looked.

During the above, ZAC *looks in just for this exchange with* JAKE.

ZAC.
Good work, Jake.

JAKE.
I'd be OK if my hands didn't shake.

JACINTA *comes off the phone.*

JACINTA.
Good work, Jake. The franchise I got from Corman – what a pig –
I sell of course to some American.
You will arrange it, no wonder I am so fond,
And I put the money in a delicious Eurobond,
Yumyum.
I think that is all.
One more phone call,
Then I go see Biddulph, the white knight –
But you don't mention this to Zac, all right?

JAKE.
This deal's not enough?

JACINTA.
What is enough?
Don't worry, Jake, you're making it.
Just keep on, taking and taking and taking it.

JAKE.
I do.

JACINTA *phones a shop.*

JACINTA.
I like to order a tree. Maybe twenty feet tall. Fig, walnut, banyan? Lemon, yes that's sweet.
Send it please to Zac Zackerman, Klein Merrick, and a card saying 'to Zac with love from Jacinta until we meet'.

DUCKETT *and* BIDDULPH. BIDDULPH *has a newspaper.*

BIDDULPH.
Now Duckett, your image gets better and better.
Have you seen this letter?

DUCKETT.
No, show me the letter.

BIDDULPH.
MPs of all parties and union leaders,
Teachers and lawyers and ordinary readers
All hope you'll succeed

DUCKETT.
Oh let's have a read.

BIDDULPH.
In stopping the raider who just wants a profit.

DUCKETT.
But we want a profit.

BIDDULPH.

We will make a profit.
But at the right time and in the right place,
With a smile on our very acceptable face.
You do so much good, you give so much enjoyment –

DUCKETT.
Youth unemployment.

BIDDULPH.

Yes, youth unemployment,
Swimming pools, pensioners, toy libraries, art –

DUCKETT.
What's this about art?

BIDDULPH.

You don't give a fart,
I know it, they know it, you just mustn't show it,
We're doing so well, Duckett, don't you dare blow it.
You've commissioned a mural called Urban and Rural,
It's sixty feet high –

DUCKETT.

I've commissioned a mural?

BIDDULPH.
And tomorrow you're joining the scouts for a hike.

DUCKETT.
I'm not sure I like –

BIDDULPH.

You go for a hike.
Your picture will be on the front of the *Mail*.
And we really can't fail.

DUCKETT.

You're sure we can't fail?
Sometimes I dream that I'll end up in jail.

BIDDULPH.
But you've done nothing wrong, you're an innocent victim,
Corman's the villain, you'll see when we've licked him.
He's sure to be up to some terrible schemes.

DUCKETT.
I just have bad dreams.

BIDDULPH.

Well don't have bad dreams.

DUCKETT.
I've done nothing wrong, I'm an innocent victim.

BIDDULPH.
And Corman will lose because we have tricked him.
Now we're meeting Señora Condor.
What the hell's she want I wonder.

JACINTA CONDOR *arrives*.

JACINTA.
Mr Duckett. Miss Biddulph. As a major shareholder I have been wondering whether I should accept Corman's offer.

BIDDULPH.
You don't want to do that, Señora Condor.

JACINTA.
I was hoping you could help me to make up my mind. I don't know how much you know about my country.

BIDDULPH.
It's really absurd, from what I have heard,
You bear an intolerable burden of debt.

JACINTA.
My country is poor, it can't stand much more,
I really can see no solution just yet.
When I wish to borrow, much to my sorrow,
The banks here in Britain are overextended.

BIDDULPH.
I think they might lend a small sum to a friend,
And we hope this sad period is very soon ended.

JACINTA.
You think your bank will lend me money?

BIDDULPH.
I think if I explain the special circumstances it could probably be arranged.

JACINTA.
Señora Biddulph
You are pleased with yourself
And certainly so you ought.
And ah Señor Duckett
You don't know your luck, it
Is now my decision you get my support.

DUCKETT.
We get her support?

BIDDULPH.
Just as we ought.

DUCKETT.
I sometimes have dreams that I'll end up in court.

JACINTA.
And now do you think it is time for a drink?

BIDDULPH.
Time for a drink!

DUCKETT.
What do you think, Biddulph?

BIDDULPH.
I'm telling you, Duckett.
I begin to think fuck it.
Pull yourself together.

MERRISON *and* MARYLOU BAINES *at* MARYLOU'*s office in New York.*

MERRISON.
So I've had three years pretty much in the wilderness.
I've had a great time skiing with my kids.
I've bred Tennessee walking horses. But I guess
Banking's in my blood. I miss the bids,
I miss the late nights, I miss the gambles.
So now I've gotten my own operation.
I can't forgive Durkfeld for the shambles
He's made of Klein Merrick. A great nation
Needs great enterprises, not black plastic
And grey lino and guys in polyester.
(I just bought a Matisse for seven million dollars, could have hung in the boardroom.)

MARYLOU.
I guess the old wound's beginning to fester.
It's about time you did something drastic.
Go for it, Jack. Why don't you sabotage
Durkfeld's deals? I've got a lot of stocks
Coming and going here in arbitrage
Should enable you to give him a few knocks.

MERRISON.
He's got his fingers in a lot of pies.

MARYLOU.
In the UK there's Corman Enterprise.

MERRISON.
You think I should step in as a white knight?

MARYLOU.
No, that's already happening all right.
Wouldn't it be far wittier to make
Corman himself a target?

MERRISON.
I'll buy a stake
In Corman straight away. I'll get some little
Nogood company run by a real punk
To take it over with a lot of junk.
I'd really like to see Durkfeld in the hospital.
Do you happen to have any Corman stock available?

MARYLOU.
Yes, I kind of thought it might be saleable.
How much do you want?

MERRISON.
How much have you got?

MARYLOU.
Let's talk to TK.

MERRISON *goes.*

TK? Sell Mr Merrison all the Corman we've got.
And buy all you can get straight away.
He'll give us a good price and take the lot.

TK.
OK.

SCILLA *and* GRIMES *playing Pass the Pigs.*

SCILLA.
Grimes and I were having a glass of poo and playing Pass the Pig,
Where you throw little pigs like dice. It's a good way to unwind
Because when trading stops you don't know what to do with your mind.

GRIMES.
Trotter!

SCILLA.
Except my mind was also full of Jake and how he'd been up to something big.

GRIMES.
Razorback, snouter. Fucking pig out.

I knew Jake was up to something but I'd never have guessed that was what it was about.

SCILLA.
He might have made a million. Trotter. Razorback.

GRIMES.
Marylou Baines! And he's in on it somehow, Zac.
Did he leave a will?

SCILLA.
I don't know.

GRIMES.
Trotter, snouter.
Fucking nuisance if he's died without a
Will, / fucking lawyers

SCILLA.
Daddy and I are next of kin.

GRIMES.
Will you marry me?

SCILLA.
Leave it out Grimes.

GRIMES.
Double snouter. I think I'm going to win.
I once threw double snouter three times.

SCILLA.
Are we playing a pound a point?

GRIMES.
Snouter, trotter.
There's the money he's made already. There's a lot o'
Money still owing him, bound to be,
And why can't that be collected by you and me?
It's just a matter of tracing his contacts, innit.
They'll want him replacing. / Snouter!

SCILLA.
You'll pig out in a minute.
There's someone who killed him.

GRIMES.
Risks are there to be taken.
Trotter, jowler. Fuckit, makin' bacon.
Do I lose all my points for the whole game?

SCILLA.
Yes, Grimes, isn't it a shame.

And I've got forty-five. Trotter, fifty. / Snouter, sixty. Double razorback, eighty. Hell, I've pigged out. Back to forty-five.

GRIMES.
I'd have some questions for Jake if he was alive.
What about your old man?

SCILLA.
Denies he got a single tip.

GRIMES.
I bet he knows more / than he lets on.

SCILLA.
He'll be so pissed by now he might let something slip.

GRIMES.
He may know where Jake stashed the loot.

SCILLA.
Let's go round there now and put in the boot.
Really, this morning he couldn't have been fouler.
Let's drive / there now.

GRIMES.
Double leaning jowler!
Double leaning jowler as I live and breathe!

SCILLA.
He's so two-faced you don't know what to believe.
We'll make him talk.

GRIMES.
I'm winning! Double fucking leaning jowler!

SCILLA.
Bring the pigs.

GREVILLE *and* FROSBY *at* GREVILLE*'s house. Drinking.*

GREVILLE.
It's times like this you need an old friend.
We haven't seen each other for a while,
I blame myself but know that in the end
It's only you that travels that last mile.
It helps so much to have someone I'm fond
Of here to sit and drink and share my grief.
There's no one else I'm sure his word's his bond.
Talking things over gives me such relief.

FROSBY.
Greville, there's something –

GREVILLE.
Poor Jake. You knew him as a little lad.
Remember the wooden soldier you once made him?

FROSBY.
Greville, there's something –

GREVILLE.
He wasn't really bad.
Some bastard whizzkid probably betrayed him.
Poor Jakey, how could anybody sell you?

FROSBY.
Greville, there's something that I ought to tell you.

SCILLA *and* GRIMES *arrive.*

SCILLA.
Daddy!

GREVILLE.
Scilla!

SCILLA.
Grimes, a colleague. My dad. Mr Frosby.

GRIMES.
Nice place you've got. High ceilings. Plenty of headroom.
Room for a chandelier. How many bedrooms?

GREVILLE.
Six, actually, now that you come to mention –

GRIMES.
That's all right. I could always build an extension.

GREVILLE.
It's not for sale.

GRIMES.
No, I was just thinking.
I'd give you half a million.

GREVILLE.
What are you drinking?

SCILLA.
Daddy. Tell me the truth if you're sober en –
ough to talk properly. About Jake.

GRIMES.
I'd get an alsatian and a doberman.

GREVILLE.
Darling, I think you're making a mistake.

SCILLA.
Do I know more than you? Marylou Baines.
Yes?

GREVILLE.
Now Scilla –

SCILLA.
Don't think you can smile a
Lot and not tell me. Ill gotten gains,
Right? Millions!

GRIMES.
I'll get a rottweiler.

SCILLA.
And nobody told me.

GREVILLE.
I know nothing about –

SCILLA.
Nothing?

GREVILLE.
Scilla, there's no need to shout.
Of course my son would make the odd suggestion –

SCILLA.
Where's his money?

GREVILLE.
But there's no question –
Marylou Baines?

GRIMES.
A rottweiler's a killer.

SCILLA.
What about me?

GREVILLE.
I protected you, Scilla.
It's bad enough to see a woman get work
Without her being part of an old boy network.

SCILLA.
Fuck off. I want my share.

GREVILLE.
Your share of what?
Daddy's always given you all he's got.
My little girl! Jake seems to have been much bigger
Than poor old daddy knew. If it's as you say,

If we're really dealing with a six nought figure.
Where the hell's he hidden it away?

GRIMES.
Don't piss about. We haven't got all day.
Who's his solicitor?

GREVILLE.
I'm afraid I don't –

GRIMES.
Who's his accountant?

GREVILLE.
In any case I won't –

FROSBY.
Who is this? An awful lout.

GRIMES.
If he really don't know we should get back.

FROSBY.
Ordering everyone about.

GRIMES.
It might be more use talking to Zac.

SCILLA.
If you're holding out on me daddy you'll be sorry.

GRIMES.
We'll have your feet run over by a lorry.

FROSBY.
Who is this horrible young vandal?
I don't need to know his name.
Responsible for all the scandal.
He's the one you ought to blame.

GRIMES.
You've all been coining it for years.

FROSBY.
My lovely city's sadly changed.
Sic transit gloria! Glory passes!
Any wonder I'm deranged,
Surrounded by the criminal classes.

GRIMES.
You've all been coining it for years.
All you fuckwits in the City.
It just don't look quite so pretty,

All the cunning little jobs,
When you see them done by yobs.

FROSBY.
He's the one you ought to blame.

GRIMES.
We're only doing just the same
All you bastards always done.
New faces in your old square mile,
Making money with a smile,
Just as clever, just as vile.

GREVILLE.
No, he's right, you killed my son.

GRIMES.
All your lives you've been in clover,
Fucking everybody over,
You just don't like to see us at it.

GREVILLE.
Scilla, I forbid you to associate with this oik.

SCILLA.
Daddy, you're trading like a cunt.
This is a waste of time. I'm going to see Corman again.

GREVILLE.
Scilla, wait, if you find out about Jake's money –

SCILLA.
Don't worry, I won't tell you, I'll protect you.

GREVILLE.
Scilla –

GRIMES.
If you want to sell the house I can pay cash.

SCILLA *and* GRIMES *leave.*

GREVILLE.
Because of yobs like him my Jake was led astray.
If it wasn't for that bastard he'd be alive today.
It's times like this you need an old friend –

FROSBY.
Greville.
It's me that told the DTI.
I can't quite remember why.
It didn't occur to me he'd die.

ZAC.

ZAC.
That afternoon things were going from bad to worse.
Jake was dead and I'd just as soon it was me they'd taken off in a hearse.
I'd just discovered Jacinta and Ajibala were no fucking help at all,
And I find Scilla hanging about in the hall.

ZAC *and* SCILLA *outside* CORMAN'*s office.*

SCILLA.
Zac, I want to see Corman. Get me in.

ZAC.
Don't talk to me. We may not even win.
Jacinta Condor's supporting Biddulph which may wreck
The whole deal, and Nigel Ajibala's done god knows what with a two million pound cheque.

SCILLA.
Jacinta Condor? Nigel Ajibala?

ZAC.
I've got to get this sorted / before Corman finds out.

SCILLA.
But they were in Jake's diary.

ZAC.
Scilla, don't shout.

SCILLA.
Would either of them be likely to kill
Jake? Or more important still
Could they tell me about his bank account?
Which bank is it in? / And what's the total amount?

ZAC.
They've kicked this dog of a deal when I hoped they'd pat it. /
I've got to find them.

SCILLA.
And if it's in a numbered Swiss account, Zac, how do I get at it?

ZAC *goes.* MELISSA, *a model, enters.*

SCILLA.
Are you going to see Mr Corman?

MELISSA.
I don't know his name.
I'm having a picture taken. The PR
Consultant is in there with him, she's called Dolcie Starr.

Last time I did a job like this the bastard put his hand on my crutch.
I was ready to walk out, I said, 'What's your game?'
I hope nothing like that –

SCILLA.
Can I go instead of you?

MELISSA.
How much?

CORMAN *and* DOLCIE STARR, *a PR consultant.*

CORMAN.
My image is atrocious. 'Profiteering.'
'Decline of British Industry.' 'Robber gangs.'
There's even a cartoon here where I'm leering
At an innocent girl called Albion and I've got fangs.
I want to be seen as Albion's Mr Right.
I need to be transformed overnight.
Can you make me look as good as Duckett?

STARR.
No, I'm afraid he's completely cornered the market
In fatherly, blue-eyed, babies, workers' friend,
Someone on whom the CBI can depend –

CORMAN.
I'm all that.

STARR.
No, you're none of that.

CORMAN.
Shit.

STARR.
Cheer up, Corman, you're the opposite.

CORMAN.
Then what am I paying you good money for?

STARR.
Let Duckett be good. And a bore.
Then you can be bad. And glamorous.
You'll have top billing by tonight.
Everyone loves a villain if he's handled right. /
Bad has connotations of amorous.

CORMAN.
Bad and glamorous?

STARR.
Two dimensions, spiritual and physical. First, spiritual.
CORMAN.
That's Duckett's area. He's a lay preacher. /
You don't want me to be a Moslem?
STARR.
No, secular spiritual. Arts. For you to reach a
Wide audience it's absolutely essential /
You sponsor –
CORMAN.
Duckett sponsors arts.
STARR.
He sponsors provincial
Orchestras. You need the National
Theatre for power, opera for decadence,
String quartets bearing your name for sensitivity and elegance,
And a fringe show with bad language for a thrill.
That should take care of the spiritual.
Now the physical. It's a pity you haven't a yacht.
CORMAN.
I'll buy one now.
STARR.
No, we'll work with what we've got.
I do recommend a sex scandal.
CORMAN.
Sex scandal? / That's the last thing –
STARR.
Will you let me handle this?
You think because you're already scandalous /
In the financial –
CORMAN.
I don't want –
STARR.
But that's the point. Fight scandal with scandal.
We provide a young girl who'll say you did it eight times a night.
Your wife is standing by you, so that's all right. /
CORMAN.
(I'm not married.)
STARR.
There could be a suggestion the girl might take her life –
If necessary we provide the wife.

CORMAN.
I'm not sure –

STARR.
There's ugly greedy and sexy greedy, you dope.
At the moment you're ugly which is no hope.
If you stay ugly, god knows what your fate is.
But sexy greedy *is* the late eighties.

CORMAN.
What about Aids? I thought sexy was out.

STARR.
The more you don't do it, the more it's fun to read about.
We might have made you make a statement about taking care.
Wicked and responsible, the perfect chair / man.

CORMAN.
I don't think I –

STARR.
We can take the pictures straightaway. / Melissa!

CORMAN.
Pictures?

STARR.
You don't have to do a thing, not even kiss her.

SCILLA *comes in.*

SCILLA.
Melissa's ill. I'm Scilla, the replacement.

STARR.
Mr Corman, you need to stand more adjacent.

CORMAN.
I can't stop working while you take pictures. Zac!
Where the fuck's he gone and why isn't he back?

He recognises SCILLA.

You again?

SCILLA *and* CORMAN *talk while* STARR *takes photographs.*

SCILLA.
I've important news for you about Albion,
If you'll tell me more about Jake.

CORMAN.
What news?

SCILLA.
Jacinta Condor?

CORMAN.
What about her?
SCILLA.
How much did he make?
STARR.
Please look fonder.
SCILLA.
How much did you pay him?
CORMAN.
Two hundred grand.
SCILLA.
What did he do with it?
STARR.
If you took her hand.
CORMAN.
What about the señora?
SCILLA.
She's supporting Biddulph's bid.
STARR.
Could you be more a-
ffectionate – keep still please. Please smile. Smile, kid.
CORMAN.
I'll kill the bitch. /
I knew there was something funny.
SCILLA.
He was so fucking rich.
Who else gave him money?
CORMAN.
What else? Is that the lot?
SCILLA.
Ajibala.
CORMAN.
What? what?
SCILLA.
More about Jake, or I won't say a word.
CORMAN.
I could name six companies he's dealt with, four merchant banks and two MPs and that's only what I've heard.
Your brother was widely respected in the City.
Now what about Ajibala? have some pity.

SCILLA.

I'll tell you about him for a small fee.
Three companies, two banks and one MP.

CORMAN *whispers to* SCILLA. STARR *snaps enthusiastically.*

STARR.

That's the way. That's what we like to see.
Look as if you're having a lot of fun.
We'll have the front page story of the *Sun*.

SCILLA.

Ajibala's gone off with the two million you gave him.

CORMAN.

Not bought my stock? There's nothing going to save him, Zac!

He realises about the pictures.

CORMAN.

Hang on a minute, you can't use these, this girl is the sister of the dead whizzkid in today's papers.

STARR.

And that's a scandal with which you've got no connection?

CORMAN.

No, that's the scandal where there is a connection but I don't want it known, I just want to be connected with the fictitious scandal where I've got a permanent erection.
(Eight times a night? Maybe four, let's be plausible.)

STARR.

But we can't let the whole story escape us.
This other scandal's a high-profile thriller.
Terrific pictures. / What's your name? Scilla?

CORMAN.

No, please –

SCILLA.

What's this about eight times a night?

STARR.

You make a statement to the press saying –

SCILLA.

Right. Keep paying or I'll agree.
Three companies.

CORMAN *whispers to* SCILLA.

Two banks.

CORMAN *whispers.*

One MP.

CORMAN *whispers.*

SCILLA.
I've never seen Mr Corman before.
From what I do see he's an awful bore.

CORMAN.
Great! More! more! Don't skimp.

SCILLA.
He's physically repellent. What a wimp.

STARR.
Ok Ok, I get it. What duplicity.
Why don't you people appreciate publicity?
You've wasted a lot of film. Where's Melissa?

STARR *leaves.*

CORMAN.
Do you want a job? Most of the people who work for me are mentally defective.

SCILLA.
Maybe later when I've finished being a detective.

CORMAN.
Zac! Etherington!
I want blood. What the fuck's going on?

ZAC *comes in followed by* NIGEL AJIBALA.

ZAC.
Hold on, I've got Ajibala right here.

CORMAN. Where's my money? You'd better start talking fast.
You can stick your cocoa beans up your arse.
Where's my two million pounds?

NIGEL.
I'm delighted to have this opportunity
Of explaining how by judicious speculation
I plan to increase the sum that you gave me so that I can buy even more shares in support of your acquisition.
I think I may certainly say with impunity /
That when you –

ETHERINGTON *comes in with* GREVETT, *a DTI inspector.*

CORMAN.
Ajibala, I've been tricked.

I gave you two million pounds / on the strict
Understanding that you'd –

ETHERINGTON.
Mr Corman. Mr Corman. Mr Corman.

GREVETT.
Do finish your sentence, Mr Corman.

CORMAN.
What's going on? Who the hell's this?
Who let him in? Sack the receptionist.

GREVETT.
I identified myself to your receptionist
As Grevett from the Department of Trade and Industry. /
People don't usually refuse to see me.

CORMAN.
Very nice to meet you, Mr Grevett.

ETHERINGTON.
I assured Mr Grevett we'd be delighted to assist
With his inquiries in any way we could. /
We know the DTI is a force for good.

CORMAN.
Delighted.

GREVETT.
What was that about two million pounds?

ETHERINGTON.
I thought it might interest you, because it sounds /
Unusual, but in fact –

CORMAN.
What was it, Zac?

ZAC.
Mr Corman is paying Klein Merrick, the bank I work for, two million pounds for advisory /
Services.

ETHERINGTON.
The sum's derisory /
Considering the immense –

GREVETT.
I believed he was addressing this gentleman?

ETHERINGTON.
By no means.

CORMAN.
Mr Ajibala, who supplies our cocoa beans.

GREVETT.
So the sum in question was to do with the cocoa trade?

ZAC *and* ETHERINGTON.
No.

CORMAN (*simultaneously*).
Yes. That is no, but we have made
Some arrangements to do with cocoa which were being discussed.

ETHERINGTON.
But the two million pounds was a payment to Klein.

ZAC.
Yes, that side of the business is all mine.

GREVETT.
Mr Ajibala, you can confirm I trust
That you never received the sum of two million?

NIGEL.
I only wish I had.

All laugh except GREVETT.

GREVETT.
The suggestion seems to cause you some amusement.
I have to establish you see that no inducement
Financial or otherwise was offered by Mr Corman
To buy stock to help support his price.

NIGEL.
Two million pounds would be extremely nice.
But no, Mr Grevett, I assure you.
An account of the cocoa trade would only bore you.

GREVETT.
And you Mr Corman would confirm – ?

CORMAN. Absolutely.

GREVETT.
It sounded as if you were asking him to return
Two million pounds. I must have misunderstood.
You weren't asking – ?

CORMAN.
No, no no, why should I?
I never gave him a two million pound cheque.

NIGEL.
So naturally he can't ask for it back.

I must be going. I've meetings to attend.
Good afternoon, Mr Corman.

CORMAN.
Wait.

GREVETT.
What?

CORMAN.
Nothing.

SCILLA *waylays* NIGEL *on his way out.*

SCILLA.
I've got to talk to you. You were a friend
Of my brother Jake.

NIGEL.
Who? I never met him.

SCILLA.
It seems to be very easy to forget him.
Do you owe him money?

NIGEL.
This is crazier and crazier.
If you'll excuse me I have a very important meeting about cocoa stocks in Malaysia.

NIGEL AJIBALA *leaves.*

GREVETT.
Does the name Jake Todd ring a bell?

CORMAN.
No. Oh yes, in the paper. Most unfortunate.
(I hope the stupid bastard rots in hell.)

GREVETT.
Not someone with whom you were personally acquainted?

CORMAN.
No, not at all. He seems to have been tainted /
By allegations of –

GREVETT.
I don't wish to be importunate,
But I was wondering if it would be possible for me to cast an eye
Over any papers relating to your interest in Albion, just a formality.

CORMAN.
This way.

GREVETT.
Your involvement, Mrs Etherington, naturally goes a long way to reassure us of the transaction's total legality.

ETHERINGTON.
There could of course be aspects of which I wasn't aware because my participation wasn't required.

CORMAN.
Etherington, you're fired.

GREVETT *and* ETHERINGTON *leave.*

CORMAN.
We'll give him a pile of papers ten feet high
And keep him busy till after the deal's completed.
Fuck the DTI, Zac, I refuse to be defeated.
I don't care if I go to jail, I'll win whatever the cost.
They may say I'm a bastard but they'll never say I lost.

ZAC.
Corman, there's one thing.
Gleason called and said he's seeing *Lear* at the National.
Could you meet him and have a word at the interval.
I don't know why you're being asked to meet a cabinet minister,
I hope it's nothing sinister.
But when the government asks you for a date, you don't stand them up.

CORMAN.
Fuck.

CORMAN *leaves.* ZAC *and* SCILLA *alone.*

ZAC.
Whether we'll get away with this is anybody's guess.
(My guess is no.)
And to think Jacinta Condor – / god, what an awful mess.

SCILLA.
She knew Jake, didn't she? Ajibala denied it.

ZAC.
He's the key to all the deals, of course they're going to hide it.

SCILLA.
I want to meet them.

ZAC.
Scilla, we all have to lie low.

SCILLA.
I want to meet all his contacts because someone's going to know where / his money is.

ZAC.
It'll be in a nominee company, and god knows where, no one except maybe Marylou Baines might know.

SCILLA.
Then I'll go and see Marylou Baines. / She's the one who made him.

ZAC.
No Scilla, I didn't mean –

SCILLA.
Yes, she'll know where his money is because she'll know how she paid him.
Do you think she owes him money? / Maybe I could collect.

ZAC.
Scilla –

SCILLA.
I'll go to New York / tonight.

ZAC.
Scilla, we must keep out of the news.
If you're going to be stupid I'll call Marylou and warn her and she'll refuse –

SCILLA.
How much does Mr Grevett of the DTI suspect?
I could go and have a word / with him

ZAC.
Scilla, don't be absurd.

SCILLA.
I could have my picture in the papers
With Corman alleging all kinds of capers /
And linking him publicly with bad Jake Todd.

ZAC.
Scilla, you wouldn't. God.

SCILLA.
So call Marylou Baines and tell her I'm on my way to Heathrow and she's to see me. Do it.

ZAC.
At least you'll be out of England.

SCILLA.
I'll send you a postcard.

ZAC.
Scilla, I thought you were some kind of English rose.

SCILLA.
Go stick the thorns up your nose, bozo.

SCILLA *goes.*

ZAC.
Somewhere along the line I really blew it.

MERRISON *and* SOAT, *President of Missouri Gumballs, at a drugstore in Missouri.*

MERRISON.
So how would you like to acquire a multinational?

SOAT.
Mr Merrison, this hardly seems rational.
My company is really extremely small.
You realise our only product is those little balls
Of gum you buy in the street out of machines?
If Corman took me over, I'd understand it.
But I'm really not cut out for a corporate bandit.
I've hardly got out from under my last creditor
And now you're trying to turn me into a predator.

MERRISON.
The smaller you are, the bigger the triumph for me.
I can raise four billion dollars of junk.

SOAT.
Mr Merrison. I'm afraid I'm in a funk.
I don't know what to say. What're you doin'?

MERRISON.
I'm using you, Mr Soat, to humiliate
Somebody I have good reason to hate.

SOAT.
I'm not sure –

MERRISON.
I wouldn't like to ruin
Missouri Gumballs, it seems kind of dumb.

SOAT.
No no. No no no no. Don't take my gum.
I'll think about it. I've thought about it. Great.

CORMAN, GLEASON, *a cabinet minister, in the interval at the National Theatre.*

GLEASON.
Enjoying the show?

CORMAN.

I'm not watching it.

GLEASON.

It's excellent of course, they're not botching it.
But after a hard day's work my eyes keep closing.
I keep jerking awake when they shout.

CORMAN.

It's hard to follow the plot if you keep dozing. /
What exactly is this meeting all about?

GLEASON.

Yes, Goneril and Reagan and Ophelia –
Good of you to come.
We have here two conflicting interests.
On the one hand it's natural the investor
Wants to make all the profit that he can,
And institutions' duty to the pensioners
Does put the onus on the short-term plan.
On the other hand one can't but help mention
The problems this creates for industry,
Who needs long-term research and development
In order to create more employment.
It's hard to reconcile but we must try.

CORMAN.

I totally agree with the CBI.
Long-term issues mustn't be neglected.
The responsibility of management –

GLEASON.

We – by which I mean of course the government –
Recognise that alas nothing's perfect.
That's something you learn in politics.
We want to cut the top rate of tax,
And profit related pay's a good incentive.
But we do think things have gone too far
In the quick-profit short-term direction.
We wouldn't interfere in a free market.
But we are of course approaching an election.

CORMAN.

Absolutely and I hope to give
More than moral support to the party.
I've always been a staunch Conservative.

GLEASON.

My dear fellow, nobody doubts your loyalty.

That's why I have so little hesitation
In asking this small service to the nation.
Drop your bid. Give up. Leave it alone.

CORMAN.
Out of the question. Sorry. Out of the question.

GLEASON.
I absolutely appreciate the problem –

CORMAN.
Leave me alone will you to do my job.

GLEASON.
I'm sorry, Corman, but I must forbid it.
A takeover like this in the present climate
Makes you, and the City, and us look greedy.
Help us be seen to care about the needy.
Help us to counteract the effect of Tebbit.

CORMAN.
What if I say no?

GLEASON.
I wouldn't like to dwell on the unsavoury
Story of that young man's suicide –

CORMAN.
Are you threatening me?

GLEASON.
I do admire your bravery.
No, but my colleagues in the DTI
Did, I believe, call on you today.

CORMAN.
Leave it out, Gleason, I've had enough.
DTI? I'm going to call your bluff.
If my takeover's going to hurt your image
Another scandal would do far more damage

GLEASON.
Mr Corman, I'll be brutally frank.
A scandal would not be welcomed by the Bank
Nor will it be tolerated by the Tories.
Whenever you businessmen do something shitty
Some of it gets wiped off on the City,
And the government's smelly from the nasty stories.

Meanwhile, 'Ladies and gentlemen take your seats' etc.

CORMAN.
Us businessmen? / The banks are full of crap.

GLEASON.
So if you persist and make a nasty mess
Not a single bank will handle your business.

CORMAN.
You can't do that, Gleason, don't make me laugh.

GLEASON.
Corman, please, don't make my patience snap.
I wouldn't want to miss the second half.
You drop your bid. We stop the DTI.

CORMAN.
You'd stop the scandal breaking anyway.
Are you telling me you can't control the press?

GLEASON.
Yes, but we'd break you. Do you want to try?
You drop the bid. We stop the DTI.

CORMAN.
Why pick on me? Everyone's the same.
I'm just good at playing a rough game.

GLEASON.
Exactly, and the game must be protected.
You can go on playing after we're elected.
Five more glorious years free enterprise,
And your services to industry will be recognised.

GLEASON *goes.*

CORMAN.
Cunt. Right. Good.
At least a knighthood.

ZAC *and* JACINTA, *exhausted, in the foyer of the Savoy.*

ZAC.
So he cancelled the deal.

JACINTA.
And how do you feel?

ZAC.
Exhausted.

JACINTA.
I get you a drink.
At least we can meet,
You're not rushed off your feet,
It's better like this I think.

ZAC.
Jacinta, I still can't forgive you for going to Biddulph, the whole deal could have been wrecked.

JACINTA.
But I get more money that way, Zac, really what do you expect?
I can't do bad business just because I feel romantic.

ZAC.
The way you do business, Jacinta, drives me completely frantic.

JACINTA.
I love the way you are so obsessed when you're thinking about your bids.

ZAC.
I love that terrible hospital scam / and the drug addicted kids.

JACINTA.
(That's true, Zac!)
I love the way you never stop work, I hate a man who's lazy.

ZAC.
The way you unloaded your copper mines drove me completely crazy.

JACINTA.
Zac, you're so charming, I'm almost as fond
Of you as I am of a eurobond.

ZAC.
I thought we'd never manage to make a date.
You're more of a thrill than a changing interest rate.

JACINTA.
This is a very public place to meet.

ZAC.
Maybe we ought to go up to your suite.

They get up to go.

ZAC.
Did you ever play with a hoop when you were a child and when it stops turning it falls down flat?
I feel kind of like that.

JACINTA.
I am very happy. My feeling for you is deep.
But will you mind very much if we go to sleep?

GREVILLE, *drunk*.

GREVILLE.

Maybe I should retire while my career is at its pinnacle.
Working in the City can make one rather cynical.
When an oil tanker sank with a hundred men the lads cheered because they'd make a million.
When Sadat was shot I was rather chuffed because I was long of gold bullion.

Life's been very good to me. I think I'll work for Oxfam.

FROSBY, *with a gun.*

FROSBY.

I thought the sun would never set.
I thought I'd be extremely rich.
You can't be certain what you'll get.
I've heard the young say Life's a bitch.

I betrayed my oldest friend.
It didn't give me too much fun.
My way of life is at an end.
At least I have a friendly gun.
My word is my junk bond.

DAVE *and* MARTIN *have just come out of a Chinese restaurant. Late night.*

DAVE.

I've eaten too many crab claws.

MARTIN.

You'll be sick in the cab again.

DAVE.

You'll get stick from your wife again.

MARTIN.

She don't care if I'm late.

DAVE.

What's she up to then?

MARTIN.

Watch it.

DAVE.

Late city, no pity.

BRIAN, TERRY *and* VINCE *follow.*

BRIAN.

Guy meets a guy and he says what do you do for a living and he says I hurt people. / He says you hurt people,

TERRY.
Sounds like my girlfriend.

BRIAN.
he says yes I hurt people for money. / I'm a hitman.*

TERRY.
Sounds like a trader.

MARTIN.
How much was it?

DAVE.
Bet it was two fifty.

MARTIN.
Bet it was three hundred.

DAVE.
How much?

MARTIN.
Ten.

VINCE.
Two eighty five.

MARTIN.
Told you. All that crab.

DAVE *gives* MARTIN *ten pounds.*

BRIAN.
*Break a leg, five hundred pounds, break a back, a thousand /

DAVE.
I know him, he works for Liffe.

BRIAN.
And he says I'm glad I met you because my neighbour's carrying on with my wife.
So he takes him home and says see that lighted window, that's where they are, I want her dead,
How much would it cost to shoot her through the head?*

TERRY. You can't get rid of your money in Crete.
Hire every speedboat, drink till you pass out, eat
Till you puke and you're still loaded with drachs.

MARTIN. }
DAVE. } Drach attack! drach attack!

VINCE.
Why's a clitoris like a filofax?

DAVE *and* OTHERS.
Every cunt's got one.

BRIAN.
*And he says five grand.
And he says, now my neighbour what would it cost if you shot off his prick and his balls.
And he says that's five grand and all.
So he says ten grand! Yes all right, it's worth it, go on, so the hitman's stood there by the garden gate
And he points his gun at the window, and he's stood there and stood there, and he says get on with it, and the hitman says Wait.
Time it right / and I'll save you five grand.

DAVE.
I'll save you five grand.

MARTIN.
Two eurobond dealers walking through Trafalgar Square, one of them said what would you do if a bird shat on your head?
And he said /
I don't think I'd ask her out again.

DAVE.
I don't think I'd ask her out again.

SCILLA *at* MARYLOU BAINES' *office in New York.*
SCILLA, TK.

TK.
Hi, I'm TK, Marylou Baines' personal assistant.

SCILLA.
Tell Marylou Baines
I've just flown in from London, I've come here straight off the plane.
I'm Jake Todd's sister and I've got some information
That I didn't want to trust to the telephone so I've brought it myself personally to its destination.

TK.
Ms Baines won't see you I'm afraid but if you like to give me the information instead,
I'm setting up in business myself and can guarantee you'd receive service second to none because it's always those who are starting up who work hardest because they want to get ahead.
So can I help you?

SCILLA.
I didn't spend six hours crossing the Atlantic
To be fobbed off by a personal assistant.

TK.
I'm sorry about this but it is part of my job description to be resistant.

SCILLA.
I warn you, I'm very tired and I'm getting frantic,
And Marylou will get a terrible fright
Tomorrow morning if she doesn't see me tonight.

TK.
If you just give me some indication of what your problem's about –

SCILLA.
Get out of my way. OUT OUT OUT.

MARYLOU *comes in.*

MARYLOU.
So. Todd's sister. You've come flying
From London with information?

SCILLA.
No, I was lying.
You don't get information this time, Marylou.
I want to know things from you.

MARYLOU.
You can ask.

SCILLA.
I had been wondering if you killed Jake, but now I hardly care.
It's not going to bring him alive again, and the main thing's to get my share.
They left me out because I'm a girl and it's terribly unfair.
You were Jake's main employer so tell me please
How did you pay him his enormous fees?
Did somebody pass a briefcase of notes at a station under a clock?
Or did you make over a whole lot of stock?
Did he have a company and what's its name?
And how can I get in on the game?
You'll need a replacement in London who knows their way round the businesses and banks.
Can I suggest somebody?

MARYLOU.
No thanks.

SCILLA.
If you don't help me I'll go to the authorities and tell them –

MARYLOU.
Is this blackmail?

SCILLA.
Yes, of course. I can put you in jail.

MARYLOU.
I'll take the risk. I'm a risk arbitrageur.
So run off home.

TK.
And nobody in America runs better risks than her.

SCILLA.
You can stick your arbitrage up your arse.
If you don't tell me about his company
You'll find me quite a dangerous enemy.
I'm greedy and completely amoral.
I've the cunning and connections of the middle class
And I'm tough as a yob.

MARYLOU.
Scilla, don't let's quarrel.
My personal assistant's leaving. Do you want a job?

TK.
Right now?

MARYLOU.
Sure, TK, you said you wanted out,
Scilla wants in. So don't let's hang about.

MARYLOU *and* SCILLA *go.*

TK.
One thing I've learned from working for Marylou:
Do others before they can do you.

ZAC.

ZAC.
So Scilla never came back.
She sent me a postcard of the Statue of Liberty saying Bye bye Zac.
She never did find out who killed her brother but I'm sure it wasn't Corman or Jacinta or Marylou or any of us.
Who didn't want Jake to talk to the DTI? Who wanted him out of the way?
The British government, because another scandal just before the election would have been too much fuss.
So I reckon it was MI5 or the CIA.
(Or he could even have shot himself, the kid wasn't stable.)
There's bound to be endless scandals in the city but really it's incidental.

It can be a nuisance because it gives the wrong impression
And if people lose confidence in us there could be a big recession.
Sure this is a dangerous system and it could crash any minute and I sometimes wake up in bed
And think is Armageddon Aids, nuclear war or a crash, and how will I end up dead?
(But that's just before breakfast.)
What really matters is the massive sums of money being passed round the world, and trying to appreciate their size can drive you mental.
There haven't been a million days since Christ died.
So think a billion, that's a thousand million, and have you ever tried
To think a trillion? Think a trillion dollars a day.
That's the gross national product of the USA.
There's people who say the American eagle is more like a vulture.
I say don't piss on your own culture.
Naturally there's a whole lot of greed and
That's no problem because money buys freedom.
So the Tories kept the scandal to the minimum. Greville Todd was arrested and put in prison to show the government was serious about keeping the city clean and nobody shed any tears.
And the Conservatives romped home with a landslide victory for five more glorious years.
(Which was handy though not essential because it would take far more than Labour to stop us.)
I've been having a great time raising sixteen billion dollars to build a satellite,
And I reckon I can wrap it up tonight.

EVERYBODY.

SCILLA.
Scilla's been named by *Business Week* as Wall Street's rising star.

GREVILLE.
Greville walked out of the open prison but didn't get very far.

GRIMES.
Grimes does insider dealing for Scilla and Marylou (and he bought Greville's house).

JAKE.
Jake's ghost appeared to Jacinta one midnight in Peru.

JACINTA.
Jacinta marries Zac next week and they honeymoon in Shanghai.
(Good business to be done in China now.)

NIGEL.
Nigel Ajibala's doing something in Dubai.
CORMAN.
Lord Corman's helping organise the tunnel under the channel.
(He's also chairman of the board of the National Theatre.)
ETHERINGTON.
Etherington runs the City's new disciplinary panel.
DUCKETT.
Duckett had a breakdown and was given ECT.
BIDDULPH.
Biddulph's running Albion and is big in ITV.
TK.
TK ended up in jail because of some funny tricks.
MARYLOU.
Marylou Baines ran for president in 1996.
MERRISON.
Merrison's been ambassador to London, Paris, Rome.
DURKFELD.
Durkfeld had a heart attack one quiet Sunday at home.
SOAT.
Soat acquired Corman Enterprise and a dangerous reputation.
STARR.
Dolcie Starr does his PR so he's loved by the whole nation.
TERRY.
Terry went to Chicago and did a lot of coke.
VINCE.
Vince spent every penny he earned and thought it was a joke.
KATHY.
Kathy's got a telly spot, advice on buying shares.
JOANNE.
Joanne became a trader and soon she moved upstairs.
MARTIN.
Martin moved to eurobonds.
BRIAN.
Brian bought a deer park.
DAVE.
Dave went to Australia and was eaten by a shark.
FROSBY.
Frosby was forgotten.

FIVE MORE GLORIOUS YEARS

Wa-doooo do-ya-doody, wa-doooo do-ya-do
These are the best years of our lives, let wealth and favour be our guide
We can expect another five, join hands across the great divide
BACK UP: wa-doooo do-ya-doody, wa-doooo do-ya-doody
Say-wa do-ya-doody, wa-doooo do-ya-do

So raise your oysters and champagne, and as we toast the blushing bride
Pon crystal mountains of cocaine, our nostrils flare and open wide
B/U: tippy-tum-tee-tippy-tum-tum, tippy-tippy tum-tum
tippy-tum-tee-tippy-tum-tum, tippy-tippy tum-tum
say-wa tippy-tippy tum-tum
tippy-tum-tee-tippy-tum-tum, tippy-tippy tum-tum.

Chorus:
Five more glorious years, five more glorious years
B/U: we're saved from the valley of tears for five more glorious years
pissed and promiscuous the money's ridiculous
send her victorious for five fucking morious
Five more glorious years

These are the best years of our lives, with information from inside
My new Ferrari has just arrived, these pleasures stay unqualified
B/U: Fiddle diddle iddle fiddle diddie, fiddle diddle iddle
Fiddle diddle iddle fiddle diddle, fiddle diddle iddle
Say-wa fiddle diddle iddle
Fiddle-diddle-iddle-fiddle-diddle-fiddle-diddle-iddle

Chorus:
Five more glorious years, five more glorious years
B/U: we're crossing forbidden frontiers, we're sniding beneath our veneer
pissed and promiscuous, the money's ridiculous
send her victorious for five fucking morious
five more glorious years
Five more glorious years, five more glorious years
we're saved from the valley of tears for five more glorious years
pissed and promiscuous, the money's ridiculous
send her victorious for five fucking morious
five more glorious years

A capella:
These are the best years of our lives, these are the best years of our lives
These are the best years of our lives, these are the best years of our lives
B/U: wa-doooo do-ya-doody, wa-doooo do-ya-doody
Say-wa do-ya-doody, wa-doooo do-ya-do

These are the best years of our lives, and as we toast the blushing bride
My Maserati has arrived, join hands across the great divide

B/U: fiddle diddle iddle fiddle diddle, fiddle diddle iddle
fiddle diddle iddle fiddle diddle, fiddle diddle iddle
Say-wa fiddle diddle iddle
Fiddle diddle iddle- ddle diddle, fiddle diddle iddle

Chorus:
Five more glorious years, five more glorious years
B/U: we're saved from the valley of tears for five more glorious years
pissed and promiscuous, the money's ridiculous
send her victorious for five fucking morious
five more glorious years

Chorus:
Five more glorious years, five more glorious years
B/U: We're crossing forbidden frontiers for five more glorious years
pissed and promiscuous, the money's ridiculous
send her victorious for five fucking morious
five more glorious years

Notes

Cast list

a LIFFE dealer: Scilla works on the floor of the London International Financial Futures and Options Exchange. She explains what this involves on pp. 48–9. Essentially LIFFE connects those who wish to speculate on the future movements of currency and interest rates with those who wish to avoid the consequences of changes in these rates.
a commercial paper dealer: 'paper' means securities (stocks or shares), whereby a company is able to raise cash by selling a share or part of itself. Jake, as a commercial paper dealer, would handle only short-term debt and seek to gain advantage from the slightest changes in interest rates.
a gilts dealer: the British Government borrows money by issuing paper referred to as 'gilt-edged stock' to lenders in the City.
Klein Merrick: an American investment bank (the equivalent of a British merchant bank) which provides a service advising companies on how to invest and raise money.
stockbroker: an agent who buys and sells securities on behalf of clients.
jobber: buys and sells shares on their own behalf. They make their money on the difference between the buying and selling price of a stock.
arbitrageur: arbitrage involves buying securities in one country, currency or market and selling in another to take advantage of price differences. Companies practise arbitrage, but an arbitrageur is an individual who hopes to identify and buy undervalued shares just before another company makes a bid for them. Because it often relies on insider information this has become regarded as an unseemly business. Ivan Boesky, in America, was fined a hundred million dollars and banned from Wall Street for arbitrage. Marylou Baines considers the fine to be peanuts and defends Boesky (p. 38).
a corporate raider: the Billy Corman plot to take over

Albion is fully and clearly dramatised in the play – his motives, his methods, his supporters and challengers are all given clear expression: for example,

CORMAN.
Now Etherington. I want you to start a stealthy
Purchase of Albion stock. Don't frighten them.
The price must hardly move, just look quite healthy.
We'll put nooses round their necks and suddenly
tighten them. (p. 31)

a white knight: a friendly investor when a company is under threat of takeover.
DTI inspector: Department of Trade and Industry inspector – Grevett is in pursuit of Jake, having been tipped off about his providing inside information.
'The Volunteers, or The Stockjobbers': Thomas Shadwell's last play, performed at the Theatre Royal, Drury Lane, London, in 1692.

Act One

1 *Patents*: sole rights to make or sell something.
2 *the city*: the financial centre of the City of London.
Big Bang: 27 October 1986, when the Exchange's new regulations took effect and the new automated price quotation system was introduced (see p. xvi).
3 *with a multiple of 13.3*: the price is 13.3 times the profits per share.
gilts dealing room: where Government securities are bought and sold.
4 *making a tick*: making a profit from a minimal price change in the share value.
leg out of it: sell as soon as possible.
futures: securities or goods bought or sold at a fixed price for future delivery. They may be traded many times before actual delivery.
I'm lifting a leg: I'm executing one side of a trade – selling or buying, the two legs.
What are we long of?: what securities are we holding on our books at the moment? What have we got left, to sell?
5 *I'm off*: I don't want to deal.

They've been trading in a 4 tick range: just moving slightly/showing little variation in price.
poo: champagne (shampoo).
I'll be long: I'll be holding securities overnight.

6 *Doing the long end?*: he's asking over what length of time he should price the security he is holding.
If you've lost any cards: Scilla is not prepared to help Dave. Dealers used to keep cards in the top pockets of their brightly coloured jackets, on which to record sales and purchases.
an issue: a newly issued bond.
the new BFC for World Bank: a kind of bond for the World Bank.
I'll give you a level: the salesman is not buying but will advise on a price.

7 *something longer*: a date further distant.
Bundesbank: the German Central Bank (equivalent of the Bank of England).
It's a softer tone today: a quieter morning – little change.
Tokyo one month 4.28125: Tokyo interest rate for one month.

8 *crashing off*: market falling fast.
So the three month interbank sterling rate – no it's a tick under: Jake is commenting on the state of the market – the rate is slightly lower than usual.
What's with the ECU linked deposits for Nomura?: Nomura – a Japanese investment house; deposits denominated in ECUs (European Currency Unit).

11 *Sloanes*: 'Sloane Rangers' – originally denoted people who frequented the fashionable Sloane Square in London, implying rich and upper-class like Scilla.
oiks: a derogatory term for the new breed of dealer working for LIFFE, implying that they are rough and tough.
a local: a self-employed or individual trader.
conglomeration: a conglomerate is a large company with lots of disparate activities.

12 *leveraged buyouts*: a group of investors buy a company largely with borrowed money.

15 *stock options*: part of a salary package, where options are provided to buy into the company in the future, at a discounted price.

whitener: cocaine.
cartel: companies getting together to fix prices.

16 *Tokyo . . . Hong Kong*: Zac claims that England has the best living conditions of all the world financial centres.
snaffle: a simple bridle bit (referring to Greville's mount).

17 *His mouth's rather hard*: he's hard to rein in.

20 *marketmakers*: investment banks acting as wholesalers of securities.

26 *insider dealing*: dealing with inside knowledge of a company's performance – aware of information unkown to the market as a whole, which might affect the share price. This is what Jake Todd is accused of. Selling such information had recently become illegal.

27 *Eurobonds*: stocks dealt through Euroclear.
dawn raider: a dealer who buys securities at opening time, obtaining as much stock as possible, on the quiet, for a takeover of the company.

31 *Albion's price is three hundred and ten*: the buying price in pence.

32 *a leveraged management buyout*: to take over the running of their company its current management put up, say, 10% of its price; outside venture capital or bank funding provide the rest.

33 *fan club*: friends acting together, supporting a financial deal.
concert party: two or more shareholders acting together.
Metgee, Upkate, etc: obscure companies who are able to act on behalf of Corman, purchasing Albion shares.

34 *Junk bonds*: low-grade shares, issued by undistinguished investment companies, those under Grade B.
Sid: fictional investor in British Gas in TV advertisements (i.e. naive first-time buyer of shares).
overgeared: a company that has too high borrowings in relation to its assets.

39 *greenmail*: Duckett asks, should he pay the asking price to buy back Corman's shares with a loan of half a million pounds?
poison pills, shark repellent: devices employed to avoid being taken over. For example, Memorandum & Articles of Association (the constitution of a company) might give power to increase the value of existing shares, or even issue more shares to protect a company when an unfriendly

takeover is in prospect.

40 *CBI*: Confederation of British Industry.
cornering the coffee market: buying lots of coffee futures to try to force up the price.
white knight: see p. 116, i.e. friendly counter-bidder in takeover situation.

41 *Guinness*: a notorious share scandal of the 1980s, which involved the Guinness takeover bid for the Distillers Company, when the Guinness share price was manipulated to boost the value of their offer. A publicly quoted company cannot buy its own shares or induce others to do so on its behalf, which is what Guinness did. Billy Corman does this in *Serious Money*.

54 *Footsie*: FTSE 100 Share Index – the *Financial Times* list of Stock Exchange valuations for the 100 top companies.

56 *Greenhouse*: a City bar in the 1980s.

57 *iron*: iron 'oof, cockney rhyming slang for 'poof' – homosexual.

Act Two

59 *OPEC*: Organisation of Petroleum Exporting Countries.
IMF: International Monetary Fund.

60 *The official closing price*: their price at close of day.

63 *dagos . . . gringos*: dismissive racist terms referring to the South Americans and Europeans mentioned by Jacinta in her preceding speech.

66 *Bob Geldof*: pop singer famous for organising a worldwide fund-raising concert called Band-Aid on behalf of the Third World.

67 *wall game*: an outdoor ball game played only at Eton.

72 *buffer stock*: centrally held stock of a commodity, which can be used to stabilise the price.
franchise: right to sell.

73 *equity*: in this context, shares taken in lieu of repayment of loan.

77 *Contras*: a right-wing terrorist group in Nicaragua supported by the American Government.
Wall Street: Manhattan's financial district in New York, the American equivalent of the City in London. It produces the Dow Jones Indexes, the equivalent of the FTSE.

82 *Pass the Pigs*: a game in which points are scored by throwing miniature model pigs onto a board, hoping they will land in an advantageous position.
101 *junk*: junk bonds (see p. 118).
103 *Tebbit*: Norman Tebbit, Secretary of State/minister in charge of the Department of Industry – a staunch Thatcherite.
104 *the Savoy*: a top-class hotel/restaurant in central London.
107 *drachs*: Greek drachmas.
112 *ECT*: Electro-Convulsive Therapy – shock treatment for severe depression.

Questions for Further Study

1 Hamlet, talking to the Players, defines the purpose of acting as 'to hold, as 'twere, the mirror up to nature; to show virtue her own feature, scorn her own image, and the very age and body of the time his form and pressure'. How far and in what ways does *Serious Money*, first performed in 1987, fulfil Hamlet's definition of a play reflecting its times?

2 Do any of the characters in *Serious Money* attract our sympathy?

3 Are the younger generation of financial traders (Scilla/Jake/Grimes) any different to their elders (Todd/Frosby)?

4 To what extent, and in what ways, is *Serious Money* directed at the government of Mrs Thatcher? Or does it have wider application?

5 What does Caryl Churchill hope to convey by the inclusion of the extract from *The Volunteers, or The Stockjobbers* by Thomas Shadwell?

6 Is there an argument for saying that pages 111–112 are the key to the play?

7 Is the use of esoteric language, especially in the dealing scenes, a help or a hindrance to the plot and the play?

8 Is the character of Scilla as a woman, a sister, a daughter and a professional in the workplace realistically developed?

9 How does *Serious Money* in its plot and its characters illustrate the changing society in Britain in the 1980s?

10 What are the strengths and weaknesses of *Serious Money* as a play?

11 Scilla says insider dealing 'is a crime without a victim'. Does the play justify this opinion?

12 'Greed is healthy. You can be greedy and still feel good about yourself.' How far does the play reinforce this idea?

13 Can it justifiably be said that *Serious Money* is really a very slight story with minimal action and character development wrapped up in linguistic frenzy in order to attack the values of the government of the day?

14 Written a decade after the Women's Liberation Movement

was at its height, how does Caryl Churchill portray the role of women in the closed world of *Serious Money*?

15 For a profession who largely expect to be on the scrap-heap by thirty-five, can we blame the characters for their all-out rush towards success and survival. Is this a moral play?
16 What does the hunting scene contribute to the play?
17 Zackerman dismisses the British Empire as a means for Britain to buy cheap and sell at a profit. Is the world portrayed in *Serious Money* any different?
18 Does *Serious Money* deal with human nature in general or is it commenting purely on a specific place and time?
19 What are the main challenges of the play to actors and designers in the theatre?
20 Compare and contrast *Serious Money* with any other play set in a workplace.

Methuen Drama Student Editions

Jean Anouilh	*Antigone*
John Arden	*Serjeant Musgrave's Dance*
Alan Ayckbourn	*Confusions*
Aphra Behn	*The Rover*
Edward Bond	*Lear*
Bertolt Brecht	*The Caucasian Chalk Circle*
	Life of Galileo
	Mother Courage and her Children
	The Resistible Rise of Arturo Ui
	The Threepenny Opera
Anton Chekhov	*The Cherry Orchard*
	The Seagull
	Three Sisters
	Uncle Vanya
Caryl Churchill	*Serious Money*
	Top Girls
Shelagh Delaney	*A Taste of Honey*
Euripides	*Medea*
	Elektra
Dario Fo	*Accidental Death of an Anarchist*
Michael Frayn	*Copenhagen*
John Galsworthy	*Strife*
Nikolai Gogol	*The Government Inspector*
Robert Holman	*Across Oka*
Henrik Ibsen	*A Doll's House*
	Hedda Gabler
Charlotte Keatley	*My Mother Said I Never Should*
Bernard Kops	*Dreams of Anne Frank*
Federico García Lorca	*Blood Wedding*
	The House of Bernarda Alba (bilingual edition)
David Mamet	*Glengarry Glen Ross*
	Oleanna
Luigi Pirandello	*Six Characters in Search of an Author*
Mark Ravenhill	*Shopping and F***ing*
Willy Russell	*Blood Brothers*
Sophocles	*Antigone*
Wole Soyinka	*Death and the King's Horseman*
J. M. Synge	*The Playboy of the Western World*
Theatre Workshop	*Oh What a Lovely War*
Oscar Wilde	*The Importance of Being Earnest*
Tennessee Williams	*A Streetcar Named Desire*
	The Glass Menagerie
Timberlake Wertenbaker	*Our Country's Good*

Methuen Drama Modern Plays

include work by

Edward Albee
Jean Anouilh
John Arden
Margaretta D'Arcy
Peter Barnes
Sebastian Barry
Brendan Behan
Dermot Bolger
Edward Bond
Bertolt Brecht
Howard Brenton
Anthony Burgess
Simon Burke
Jim Cartwright
Caryl Churchill
Noël Coward
Lucinda Coxon
Sarah Daniels
Nick Darke
Nick Dear
Shelagh Delaney
David Edgar
David Eldridge
Dario Fo
Michael Frayn
John Godber
Paul Godfrey
David Greig
John Guare
Peter Handke
David Harrower
Jonathan Harvey
Iain Heggie
Declan Hughes
Terry Johnson
Sarah Kane
Charlotte Keatley
Barrie Keeffe
Howard Korder
Robert Lepage
Doug Lucie
Martin McDonagh
John McGrath
Terrence McNally
David Mamet
Patrick Marber
Arthur Miller
Mtwa, Ngema & Simon
Tom Murphy
Phyllis Nagy
Peter Nichols
Sean O'Brien
Joseph O'Connor
Joe Orton
Louise Page
Joe Penhall
Luigi Pirandello
Stephen Poliakoff
Franca Rame
Mark Ravenhill
Philip Ridley
Reginald Rose
Willy Russell
Jean-Paul Sartre
Sam Shepard
Wole Soyinka
Shelagh Stephenson
Peter Straughan
C. P. Taylor
Theatre de Complicite
Theatre Workshop
Sue Townsend
Judy Upton
Timberlake Wertenbaker
Roy Williams
Snoo Wilson
Victoria Wood

Methuen Drama Contemporary Dramatists

include

John Arden (two volumes)
Arden & D'Arcy
Peter Barnes (three volumes)
Sebastian Barry
Dermot Bolger
Edward Bond (six volumes)
Howard Brenton
(two volumes)
Richard Cameron
Jim Cartwright
Caryl Churchill (two volumes)
Sarah Daniels (two volumes)
Nick Darke
David Edgar (three volumes)
Ben Elton
Dario Fo (two volumes)
Michael Frayn (three volumes)
David Greig
John Godber (two volumes)
Paul Godfrey
John Guare
Lee Hall (two volumes)
Peter Handke
Jonathan Harvey
(two volumes)
Declan Hughes
Terry Johnson (two volumes)
Sarah Kane
Barrie Keefe
Bernard-Marie Koltès
David Lan
Bryony Lavery
Deborah Levy
Doug Lucie
David Mamet (four volumes)
Martin McDonagh
Duncan McLean
Anthony Minghella
(two volumes)
Tom Murphy (four volumes)
Phyllis Nagy
Anthony Nielsen
Philip Osment
Louise Page
Stewart Parker (two volumes)
Joe Penhall
Stephen Poliakoff
(three volumes)
David Rabe
Mark Ravenhill
Christina Reid
Philip Ridley
Willy Russell
Eric-Emmanuel Schmitt
Ntozake Shange
Sam Shepard (two volumes)
Shelagh Stephenson
Wole Soyinka (two volumes)
David Storey (three volumes)
Sue Townsend
Judy Upton
Michel Vinaver
(two volumes)
Arnold Wesker (two volumes)
Michael Wilcox
Roy Williams
Snoo Wilson (two volumes)
David Wood (two volumes)
Victoria Wood

For a complete catalogue of Methuen Drama titles
write to:

Methuen Drama
A & C Black Publishers Limited
38 Soho Square
London
W1D 3HB

or you can visit our website at:

www.acblack.com

CPSIA information can be obtained
at www.ICGtesting.com
Printed in the USA
LVHW041924120120
643360LV00004B/488/P